Whatever the need of the moment, the answer is to be found in Scripture, if we take the time to search for it. Whatever we're feeling, whatever we're suffering, whatever we're hoping — the Bible has something to say to us.

This collection of Bible verses is meant for use as a handy reference when you feel the need for the Bible's guidance on a particular problem in your life. It is in no way intended to replace regular Bible study or the use of a concordance for in-depth study of a subject. There are many facets of your life — and many topics in the Bible — that are not covered here.

But if you are feeling extremely lonely one day, some of the Bible's wisdom and comfort is available to you here under the topic of Loneliness. All topics are arranged alphabetically for ease of use.

All Scripture is from the New International Version of the Bible.

New International Version

THE
BIBLE
PROMISE
BOOK

BARBOUR BOOKS
Westwood, New Jersey

©1990 by Barbour and Company, Inc.

Leatherette / Mauve ISBN 1-55748-175-X
Leatherette / Blue ISBN 1-55748-176-8
Bonded Leather / Mauve ISBN 1-55748-179-2
Bonded Leather / Blue ISBN 1-55748-180-6
Bonded Leather Flexible / Mauve ISBN 1-55748-181-4
Bonded Leather Flexible / Blue ISBN 1-55748-182-2

Published by **BARBOUR AND COMPANY, INC.,**
P.O. Box 1219
Westwood, New Jersey

EVANGELICAL CHRISTIAN PUBLISHERS ASSOCIATION **ecpa** MEMBER

Typesetting by Typetronix, Inc., Cape Coral, Florida

Printed in the United States of America

New International Version

THE
BIBLE
PROMISE
BOOK

Contents

Anger

The LORD is gracious and compassionate, slow to anger and rich in love.

Psalms 145:8

. . . a forgiving God, gracious and compassionate, slow to anger and abounding in love. . . .

Nehemiah 9:17

For his anger lasts only a moment, but his favor lasts a lifetime; weeping may remain for a night, but rejoicing comes in the morning.

Psalms 30:5

My dear brothers, take note of this: Everyone should be quick to listen, slow to speak and slow to become angry, for man's anger does not bring about the righteous life that God desires.

James 1:19, 20

Do not be quickly provoked in your spirit, for anger resides in the lap of fools.

Ecclesiastes 7:9

A quick-tempered man does foolish things. . . .

Proverbs 14:17

Better a patient man than a warrior, a man who controls his temper than one who takes a city.

Proverbs 16:32

A hot-tempered man stirs up dissension, but a patient man calms a quarrel.

Proverbs 15:18

An angry man stirs up dissension, and a hot-tempered one commits many sins.

Proverbs 29:22

Refrain from anger and turn from wrath; do not fret — it leads only to evil.

Psalms 37:8

Do not make friends with a hot-tempered man, do not associate with one easily angered,

or you may learn his ways and get yourself ensnared.

Proverbs 22:24, 25

A gentle answer turns away wrath, but a harsh word stirs up anger.

Proverbs 15:1

Fathers, do not embitter your children, or they will become discouraged.

Colossians 3:21

"In your anger do not sin": Do not let the sun go down while you are still angry.

Ephesians 4:26

A man's wisdom gives him patience; it is to his glory to overlook an offense.

Proverbs 19:11

Better to live in a desert than with a quarrelsome and ill-tempered wife.

Proverbs 21:19

But I tell you that anyone who is angry with his brother will be subject to judgment.

Matthew 5:22

Get rid of all bitterness, rage and anger, brawling and slander, along with every form of malice. Be kind and compassionate to one another, forgiving each other, just as in Christ God forgave you.

Ephesians 4:31, 32

Do not take revenge, my friends, but leave room for God's wrath, for it is written: "It is mine to avenge; I will repay," says the LORD. On the contrary:
"If your enemy is hungry, feed him;
if he is thirsty, give him something to drink.
In doing this, you will heap burning coals on his head."
Do not be overcome by evil, but overcome evil with good.

Romans 12:19-21

If your enemy is hungry, give him food to eat; if he is thirsty, give him water to drink.
In doing this, you will heap burning coals on his head, and the LORD will reward you.

Proverbs 25:21, 22

My dear brothers, take note of this: Everyone should be quick to listen, slow to speak and slow to become angry, for man's anger does not bring about the righteous life that God desires.

James 1:19, 20

But now you must rid yourselves of all such things as these: anger, rage, malice, slander, and filthy language from your lips.

Colossians 3:8

Belief

"For God so loved the world that he gave his one and only Son, that whoever believes in him shall not perish but have eternal life."

John 3:16

"All the prophets testify about him that everyone who believes in him receives forgiveness of sins through his name."

Acts 10:43

As it is written:
"See, I lay in Zion a stone that causes men to stumble and a rock that makes them fall,
and the one who trusts in him will never be put to shame."

Romans 9:33

Yet to all who received him, to those who believed in his name, he gave the right to become children of God.

John 1:12

Whoever believes in him is not condemned, but whoever does not believe stands condemned already because he has not believed in the name of God's one and only Son.

John 3:18

"Whoever believes in the Son has eternal life, but whoever rejects the Son will not see life, for God's wrath remains on him."

John 3:36

For in Scripture it says:

"See, I lay a stone in Zion, a chosen and precious cornerstone,

and the one who trusts in him will never be put to shame."

1 Peter 2:6

They replied, "Believe in the Lord Jesus, and you will be saved — you and your household."

Acts 16:31

I have come into the world as a light, so that no one who believes in me should stay in darkness.

John 12:46

Then Jesus declared, "I am the bread of life. He who comes to me will never go hungry, and he who believes in me will never be thirsty."

John 6:35

" 'If you can'?" said Jesus. "Everything is possible for him who believes."

Mark 9:23

Then Jesus told him, "Because you have seen me, you have believed; blessed are those who have not seen and yet have believed."

John 20:29

I tell you the truth, he who believes has everlasting life.

John 6:47

Charity

Blessed is he who has regard for the weak; the LORD delivers him in times of trouble.

The LORD will protect him and preserve his life; he will bless him in the land and not surrender him to the desire of his foes.

Psalms 41:1, 2

He who is kind to the poor lends to the LORD, and he will reward him for what he has done.

Proverbs 19:17

"But when you give a banquet, invite the poor, the crippled, the lame, the blind, and you will be blessed. Although they cannot repay you, you will be repaid at the resurrection of the righteous."

Luke 14:13, 14

"Sell your possessions and give to the poor. Provide purses for yourselves that will not wear out, a treasure in heaven that will not be exhausted, where no thief comes near and no moth destroys."

Luke 12:33

He who despises his neighbor sins, but blessed is he who is kind to the needy.

Proverbs 14:21

Cast your bread upon the waters, for after many days you will find it again.

Ecclesiastes 11:1

He has scattered abroad his gifts to the poor, his righteousness endures forever; his horn will be lifted high in honor.

Psalms 112:9

A generous man will himself be blessed, for he shares his food with the poor.

Proverbs 22:9

Give, and it will be given to you. A good measure, pressed down, shaken together and running over, will be poured into your lap. For with the measure you use, it will be measured to you."

Luke 6:38

He who gives to the poor will lack nothing, but he who closes his eyes to them receives many curses.

Proverbs 28:27

Each man should give what he has decided in his heart to give, not reluctantly or under compulsion, for God loves a cheerful giver.

2 Corinthians 9:7

One man gives freely, yet gains even more; another withholds unduly, but comes to poverty.

A generous man will prosper; he who refreshes others will himself be refreshed.

Proverbs 11:24, 25

I was young and now I am old, yet I have never seen the righteous forsaken or their children begging bread.

They are always generous and lend freely; their children will be blessed.

Psalms 37:25, 26

And if you spend yourselves in behalf of the hungry and satisfy the needs of the oppressed, then your light will rise in the darkness, and your night will become like the noonday.

Isaiah 58:10

Command those who are rich in this present world not to be arrogant nor to put their hope in wealth, which is so uncertain, but to put their hope in God, who richly provides us with everything for our enjoyment. Command them to do good, to be rich in good deeds, and to be generous and willing to share.

1 Timothy 6:17, 18

Is it not to share your food with the hungry and to provide the poor wanderer with shelter — when you see the naked, to clothe him, and not to turn away from your own flesh and blood?

Then your light will break forth like the dawn, and your healing will quickly appear; then your righteousness will go before you, and the glory of the LORD will be your rear guard.

Isaiah 58:7, 8

So that the Levites (who have no allotment or inheritance of their own) and the aliens, the fatherless and the widows who live in your towns may come and eat and be satisfied, and so that the LORD your God may bless you in all the work of your hands.

Deuteronomy 14:29

Jesus looked at him and loved him. "One thing you lack," he said. "Go, sell everything you have and give to the poor, and you will have treasure in heaven. Then come, follow me."

Mark 10:21

"Be careful not to do your 'acts of righteousness' before men, to be seen by them. If you do, you will have no reward from your Father in heaven.

"So when you give to the needy, do not announce it with trumpets, as the hypocrites do in the synagogues and on the streets, to be honored by men. I tell you the truth, they have received their reward in full. But when you give to the needy, do not let your left hand know what your right hand is doing, so that your giving may be in secret. Then your Father, who sees what is done in secret, will reward you."

Matthew 6:1-4

"Then the King will say to those on his right, 'Come, you who are blessed by my Father; take your inheritance, the kingdom prepared for you since the creation of the world. For I was hungry and you gave me something to eat, I was thirsty and you gave me something to drink, I was a stranger and you invited me in, I needed clothes and you clothed me, I was sick and you looked after me, I was in prison and you came to visit me.'

"Then the righteous will answer him, 'LORD, when did we see you hungry and feed you, or thirsty and give you something to drink? When did we see you a stranger and invite you in, or needing clothes and clothe you? When did we see you sick or in prison and go to visit you?'

"The King will reply, 'I tell you the truth, whatever you did for one of the least of these brothers of mine, you did for me.' "

Matthew 25:34-40

Children

They replied, "Believe in the Lord Jesus, and you will be saved — you and your household."

Acts 16:31

"The promise is for you and your children and for all who are far off — for all whom the LORD our God will call."

Acts 2:39

All your sons will be taught by the LORD, and great will be your children's peace.

Isaiah 54:13

For I will pour water on the thirsty land, and streams on the dry ground;

I will pour out my Spirit on your offspring, and my blessing on your descendants.

Isaiah 44:3

When Jesus saw this, he was indignant. He said to them, "Let the little children come to me, and do not hinder them, for the kingdom of God belongs to such as these. I tell you the truth, anyone who will not receive the kingdom of God like a little child will never enter it." And he took the children in his arms, put his hands on them and blessed them.

Mark 10:14-16

Sons are a heritage from the LORD, children a reward from him.

Like arrows in the hands of a warrior are sons born in one's youth.

Blessed is the man whose quiver is full of them.

They will not be put to shame when they contend with their enemies in the gate.

Psalms 127:3-5

Your wife will be like a fruitful vine within your house; your sons will be like olive shoots around your table.

Psalms 128:3

But he lifted the needy out of their affliction and increased their families like flocks.

Psalms 107:41

They send forth their children as a flock; their little ones dance about.

Job 21:11

Children's children are a crown to the aged, and parents are the pride of their children.

Proverbs 17:6

Children's Duties

Children, obey your parents in the LORD, for this is right.

"Honor your father and mother" — which is the first commandment with a promise — "that it may go well with you and that you may enjoy long life on the earth."

Ephesians 6:1-3

Children, obey your parents in everything, for this pleases the LORD.

Colossians 3:20

" '. . . Honor your father and mother.' "

Luke 18:20

"Cursed is the man who dishonors his father or his mother."

Deuteronomy 27:16

" 'Each of you must respect his mother and father.' "

Leviticus 19:3

"Honor your father and your mother, as the LORD your God has commanded you. . . ."

Deuteronomy 5:16

My son, keep your father's commands and do not forsake your mother's teaching.

Proverbs 6:20

A wise son heeds his father's instruction, but a mocker does not listen to rebuke.

Proverbs 13:1

A fool spurns his father's discipline, but whoever heeds correction shows prudence.

Proverbs 15:5

Even a child is known by his actions, by whether his conduct is pure and right.

Proverbs 20:11

A wise son brings joy to his father, but a foolish son grief to his mother.

Proverbs 10:1

My son, if sinners entice you, do not give in to them.

Proverbs 1:10

He who keeps the law is a discerning son, but a companion of gluttons disgraces his father.

Proverbs 28:7

"Now then, my sons, listen to me; blessed are those who keep my ways.

Listen to my instruction and be wise; do not ignore it."

Proverbs 8:32, 33

My son, if your heart is wise, then my heart will be glad;

my inmost being will rejoice when your lips speak what is right.

Proverbs 23:15, 16

Listen to your father, who gave you life, and do not despise your mother when she is old.

Proverbs 23:22

The father of a righteous man has great joy; he who has a wise son delights in him.

May your father and mother be glad; may she who gave you birth rejoice!

My son, give me your heart and let your eyes keep to my ways.

Proverbs 23:24-26

Comfort

God is our refuge and strength, an ever present help in trouble.

Therefore we will not fear, though the earth give way and the mountains fall into the heart of the sea,

though its waters roar and foam and the mountains quake with their surging. *Selah*

Psalms 46:1-3

Though I walk in the midst of trouble, you preserve my life; you stretch out your hand against the anger of my foes, with your right hand you save me.

Psalms 138:7

The LORD is my rock, my fortress and my deliverer; my God is my rock, in whom I take refuge. He is my shield and the horn of my salvation, my stronghold.

Psalms 18:2

For he has not despised or disdained the suffering of the afflicted one; he has not hidden his face from him but has listened to his cry for help.

Psalms 22:24

Though he stumble, he will not fall, for the LORD upholds him with his hand.

Psalms 37:24

The Lord is good, a refuge in times of trouble.
He cares for those who trust in him.

Nahum 1:7

The salvation of the righteous comes from the Lord; he is their stronghold in time of trouble.

Psalms 37:39

Cast your cares on the Lord and he will sustain you; he will never let the righteous fall.

Psalms 55:22

"I have told you these things, so that in me you may have peace. In this world you will have trouble. But take heart! I have overcome the world."

John 16:33

"Come to me, all you who are weary and burdened, and I will give you rest."

Matthew 11:28

For just as the sufferings of Christ flow over into our lives, so also through Christ our comfort overflows.

2 Corinthians 1:5

The Lord is a refuge for the oppressed, a stronghold in times of trouble.

Psalms 9:9

For men are not cast off by the Lord forever.
Though he brings grief, he will show compassion, so great is his unfailing love.
For he does not willingly bring affliction or grief to the children of men.

Lamentations 3:31-33

Wait for the LORD; be strong and take heart and wait for the LORD.

Psalms 27:14

Contentment

A cheerful heart is good medicine, but a crushed spirit dries up the bones.

Proverbs 17:22

Keep your lives free from the love of money and be content with what you have, because God has said, "Never will I leave you; never will I forsake you."

Hebrews 13:5

All the days of the oppressed are wretched, but the cheerful heart has a continual feast.

Proverbs 15:15

A heart at peace gives life to the body, but envy rots the bones.

Proverbs 14:30

But godliness with contentment is great gain.

1 Timothy 6:6

Do not let your heart envy sinners, but always be zealous for the fear of the LORD.

There is surely a future hope for you, and your hope will not be cut off.

Proverbs 23:17, 18

Correction, God's

Because the LORD disciplines those he loves, as a father the son he delights in.

Proverbs 3:12

"Blessed is the man whom God corrects; so do not despise the discipline of the Almighty.

For he wounds, but he also binds up; he injures, but his hands also heal."

Job 5:17, 18

Blessed is the man you discipline, O LORD, the man you teach from your law;

you grant him relief from days of trouble, till a pit is dug for the wicked.

Psalms 94:12, 13

When we are judged by the LORD, we are being disciplined so that we will not be condemned with the world.

1 Corinthians 11:32

Therefore we do not lose heart. Though outwardly we are wasting away, yet inwardly we are being renewed day by day. For our light and momentary troubles are achieving for us an eternal glory that far outweighs them all.

2 Corinthians 4:16, 17

Because the LORD disciplines those he loves, and he punishes everyone he accepts as a son.

Hebrews 12:6

Our fathers disciplined us for a little while as they thought best; but God disciplines us for our good, that we may share in his holiness.

No discipline seems pleasant at the time, but painful. Later on, however, it produces a harvest of righteousness and peace for those who have been trained by it.

Hebrews 12:10, 11

Courage

Wait for the LORD; be strong and take heart and wait for the LORD.

Psalms 27:14

For the LORD loves the just and will not forsake his faithful ones.

They will be protected forever, but the offspring of the wicked will be cut off.

Psalms 37:28

But now, this is what the LORD says — he who created you, O Jacob, he who formed you, O Israel: "Fear not, for I have redeemed you; I have summoned you by name; you are mine."

Isaiah 43:1

"Don't be afraid," the prophet answered. "Those who are with us are more than those who are with them."

2 Kings 6:16

Trust in the LORD and do good; dwell in the land and enjoy safe pasture.

Psalms 37:3

He gives strength to the weary and increases the power of the weak.

Isaiah 40:29

Be strong and take heart, all you who hope in the LORD.

Psalms 31:24

I know what it is to be in need, and I know what it is to have plenty. I have learned the secret of being content in any and every situation, whether well fed or hungry, whether living in plenty or in want. I can do everything through him who gives me strength.

Philippians 4:12, 13

Death

Even though I walk through the valley of the shadow of death, I will fear no evil, for you are with me; your rod and your staff, they comfort me.

Psalms 23:4

"Where, O death, is your victory? Where, O death, is your sting?"

1 Corinthians 15:55

When calamity comes, the wicked are brought down, but even in death the righteous have a refuge.

Proverbs 14:32

Since we have now been justified by his blood, how much more shall we be saved from God's wrath through him!

Romans 5:9

Since the children have flesh and blood, he too shared in their humanity so that by his death he might destroy him who holds the power of death — that is, the devil — and free those who all their lives were held in slavery by their fear of death.

Hebrews 2:14, 15

"I tell you the truth, if a man keeps my word, he will never see death."

John 8:51

For this God is our God for ever and ever; he will be our guide even to the end.

Psalms 48:14

My flesh and my heart may fail, but God is the strength of my heart and my portion forever.

Psalms 73:26

But God will redeem my soul from the grave; he will surely take me to himself.   ***Selah***

Psalms 49:15

He will swallow up death forever.

The Sovereign LORD will wipe away the tears from all faces. . . .

Isaiah 25:8

"I will ransom them from the power of the grave; I will redeem them from death.

Where, O death, our your plagues? Where, O grave, is your destruction?

"I will have no compassion."

Hosea 13:14

Consider the blameless, observe the upright; there is a future for the man of peace.

Psalms 37:37

. . . Though outwardly we are wasting away, yet inwardly we are being renewed day by day.

23 Corinthians 4:16

That everyone who believes in him may have eternal life.

John 3:15

24

For I am convinced that neither death nor life, neither angels nor demons, neither the present nor the future, nor any powers, neither height nor depth, nor anything else in all creation, will be able to separate us from the love of God that is in Christ Jesus our Lord.

Romans 8:38, 39

Enemies

The LORD helps them and delivers them; he delivers them from the wicked and saves them, because they take refuge in him.

Psalms 37:40

"Your enemies will be clothed in shame, and the tents of the wicked will be no more."

Job 8:22

The LORD will grant that the enemies who rise up against you will be defeated before you. They will come at you from one direction but flee from you in seven.

Deuteronomy 28:7

"For the LORD your God is the one who goes with you to fight for you against your enemies to give you victory."

Deuteronomy 20:4

In famine he will ransom you from death, and in battle from the stroke of the sword.

Job 5:20

With God we will gain the victory, and he will trample down your enemies.

Psalms 60:12

"No weapon forged against you will prevail, and you will refute every tongue that accuses you.
This is the heritage of the servants of the LORD, and this is their vindication from me," declares the LORD.

Isaiah 54:17

The LORD is with me; he is my helper.
I will look in triumph on my enemies.

Psalms 118:7

To rescue us from the hand of our enemies, and to enable us to serve him without fear.

Luke 1:74

The scepter of the wicked will not remain over the land allotted to the righteous, for then the righteous might use their hands to do evil.

Psalms 125:3

For in the day of trouble he will keep me safe in his dwelling; he will hide me in the shelter of his tabernacle and set me high upon a rock. Then my head will be exalted above the enemies who surround me; at his tabernacle will I sacrifice with shouts of joy; I will sing and make music to the LORD.

Psalms 27:5, 6

When a man's ways are pleasing to the LORD, he makes even his enemies live at peace with him.

Proverbs 16:7

His heart is secure, he will have no fear; in the end he will look in triumph on his foes.

Psalms 112:8

And will not God bring about justice for his chosen ones, who cry out to him day and night? Will he keep putting them off?

Luke 18:7

If anyone does attack you, it will not be my doing; whoever attacks you will surrender to you.

Isaiah 54:15

Let those who love the LORD hate evil, for he guards the lives of his faithful ones and delivers them from the hand of the wicked.

Psalms 97:10

" 'But I will rescue you on that day, declares the LORD; you will not be handed over to those you fear. I will save you; you will not fall by the sword but will escape with your life, because you trust in me, declared the LORD.' "

Jeremiah 39:17, 18

"Rather, worship the LORD your God; it is he who will deliver you from the hand of all your enemies."

2 Kings 17:39

"Don't be afraid," the prophet answered. "Those who are with us are more than those who are with them."

2 Kings 6:16

Have no fear of sudden disaster or of the ruin that overtakes the wicked, for the LORD will be your confidence and will keep your foot from being snared.

Proverbs 3:25, 26

"All who rage against you will surely be ashamed and disgraced; those who oppose you will be as nothing and perish.

Though you search for your enemies, you will not find them.

Those who wage war against you will be as nothing at all."

Isaiah 41:11, 12

Salvation from our enemies and from the hand of all who hate us.

Luke 1:71

"For I am with you, and no one is going to attack and harm you, because I have many people in this city."

Acts 18:10

So we say with confidence, "The LORD is my helper; I will not be afraid. What can man do to me?"

Hebrews 13:6

Eternal Life

I tell you the truth, he who believes has everlasting life.

John 6:47

Jesus said to her, "I am the resurrection and the life. He who believes in me will live, even though he dies; and whoever lives and believes in me will never die. Do you believe this?"

John 11:25, 26

Listen, I tell you a mystery: We will not all sleep, but we will all be changed — in a flash, in the twinkling of an eye, at the last trumpet. For the trumpet will sound, the dead will be raised imperishable, and we will be changed. For the perishable must clothe itself with the imperishable, and the mortal with immortality. When the perishable has been clothed with the imperishable, and the mortal with immortality, then the saying that is written will come true: "Death has been swallowed up in victory."

1 Corinthians 15:51-54

And this is what he promises us — even eternal life.

1 John 2:25

For since death came through a man, the resurrection of the dead comes also through a man.

1 Corinthians 15:21

I write these things to you who believe in the name of the Son of God so that you may know that you have eternal life.

1 John 5:13

"Do not be amazed at this, for a time is coming when all who are in their graves will hear his voice and come out — those who have done good will rise to live, and those who have done evil will rise to be condemned."

John 5:28, 29

For the LORD himself will come down from heaven, with a loud command, with the voice of the archangel and with the trumpet call of God, and the dead in Christ will rise first.

1 Thessalonians 4:16

Therefore, "they are before the throne of God and serve him day and night in his temple; and he who sits on the throne will spread his tent over them.

Never again will they hunger; never again will their thirst.

The sun will not beat upon them, not any scorching heat.

For the Lamb at the center of the throne will be their shepherd; he will lead them to springs of living water.

And God will wipe away every tear from their eyes."

Revelation 7:15-17

"For God so loved the world that he gave his one and only Son, that whoever believes in him shall not perish but have eternal life."

John 3:16

So will it be with the resurrection of the dead. The body that is sown is perishable, it is raised imperishable; it is sown in dishonor, it is raised in glory; it is sown in weakness, it is raised in power; it is sown a natural body, it is raised a spiritual body.

If there is a natural body, there is also a spiritual body. So it is written: "The first man Adam became a living being"; the last Adam, a life-giving spirit. The spiritual did not come first, but the natural, and after that the spiritual.

1 Corinthians 15:42-46

And if the Spirit of him who raised Jesus from the dead is living in you, he who raised Christ from the dead will also give life to your mortal bodies through his Spirit, who lives in you.

Romans 8:11

"He will wipe every tear from their eyes. There will be no more death or mourning or crying or pain, for the old order of things has passed away."

Revelation 21:4

For the wages of sin is death, but the gift of God is eternal life in Christ Jesus our LORD.

Romans 6:23

And after my skin has been destroyed, yet in my flesh I will see God;
I myself will see him with my own eyes — I, and not another.
How my heart yearns within me!

Job 19:26, 27

The one who sows to please his sinful nature, from that nature will reap destruction; the one who sows to please the Spirit, from the Spirit will reap eternal life.

Galatians 6:8

Multitudes who sleep in the dust of the earth will awake: some to everlasting life, others to shame and everlasting contempt.

Daniel 12:2

But your dead will live; their bodies will rise.

You who dwell in the dust, wake up and shout for joy.

Your dew is like the dew of the morning; the earth will give birth to her dead.

Isaiah 26:19

Because you will not abandon me to the grave, nor will you let your Holy One see decay.

Psalms 16:10

But it has now been revealed through the appearing of our Savior, Christ Jesus, who has destroyed death and has brought life and immortality to light through the gospel.

2 Timothy 1:10

And this is the testimony: God has given us eternal life, and this life is in his Son.

1 John 5:11

Now we know that if the earthly tent we live in is destroyed, we have a building from God, an eternal house in heaven, not built by human hands.

2 Corinthians 5:1

In my Father's house are many rooms; if it were not so, I would have told you. I am going there to prepare a place for you. And if I go and prepare a place for you, I will come back and take you to be with me that you also may be where I am.

John 14:2, 3

"And this is the will of him who sent me, that I shall lose none of all that he has given me, but raise them up at the last day. For my Father's will is that everyone who looks to the Son and believes in him shall have eternal life, and I will raise him up at the last day."

John 6:39, 40

But those who are considered worthy of taking part in that age and in the resurrection from the dead will neither marry nor be given in marriage, and they can no longer die; for they are like the angels. They are God's children, since they are children of the resurrection.

Luke 20:35, 36

My sheep listen to my voice; I know them, and they follow me. I give them eternal life, and they shall never perish; no one can snatch them out of my hand.

John 10:27, 28

Whoever eats my flesh and drinks my blood has eternal life, and I will raise him up at the last day.

John 6:54

Faith

Now faith is being sure of what we hope for and certain of what we do not see.

Hebrews 11:1

. . . anyone who comes to him must believe that he exists and that he rewards those who earnestly seek him.

Hebrews 11:6

If any of you lacks wisdom, he should ask God, who gives generously to all without finding fault, and it will be given to him. But when he asks, he must believe and not doubt, because he who doubts is like a wave of the sea, blown and tossed by the wind.

James 1:5, 6

So then, just as you received Christ Jesus as LORD, continue to live in him, rooted and built up in him, strengthened in the faith as you were taught, and overflowing with thankfulness.

Colossians 2:6, 7

For it is by grace you have been saved, through faith — and this not from yourselves, it is the gift of God.

Ephesians 2:8

You are all sons of God through faith in Christ Jesus.

Galatians 3:26

But as for you, continue in what you have learned and have become convinced of, because you know those from whom you learned it, and how from infancy you have known the holy Scriptures, which are able to make you wise for salvation through faith in Christ Jesus.

2 Timothy 3:14, 15

Be on your guard; stand firm in the faith; be men of courage; be strong.

1 Corinthians 16:13

. . . the fruit of the Spirit is love, joy, peace, patience, kindness, goodness, faithfulness. . . .

Galatians 5:22

I have been crucified with Christ and I no longer live, but Christ lives in me. The life I live in the body, I live by faith in the Son of God, who loved me and gave himself for me.

Galatians 2:20

We live by faith, not by sight.

2 Corinthians 5:7

"Have faith in God," Jesus answered. "I tell you the truth, if anyone says to this mountain, 'Go throw yourself into the sea,' and does not doubt in his heart but believes that what he says will happen, it will be done for him."

Mark 11:22, 23

So that Christ may dwell in your hearts through faith. And I pray that you, being rooted and established in love, may have power, together with all the saints, to grasp how wide and long and high and deep is the love of Christ, and to know this love that surpasses knowledge — that you may be filled to the measure of all the fullness of God.

Ephesians 3:17-19

Therefore, since we are surrounded by such a great cloud of witnesses, let us throw off everything that hinders and the sin that so easily entangles, and let us run with perseverance the race marked out for us. Let us fix our eyes on Jesus, the author and perfector of our faith, who for the joy set before him endured the cross, scorning its shame, and sat down at the right hand of the throne of God.

Hebrews 12:1, 2

Faithfulness, God's

Know therefore that the LORD your God is God; he is the faithful God, keeping his covenant of love to a thousand generations of those who love him and keep his commands.

Deuteronomy 7:9

For the LORD your God is a merciful God; he will not abandon or destroy you or forget the covenant with your forefathers, which he confirmed to them by oath.

Deuteronomy 4:31

He remembers his covenant forever, the word he commanded, for a thousand generations.

Psalms 105:8

God is not a man, that he should lie, nor a son of man, that he should change his mind.

Does he speak and then not act? Does he promise and not fulfill?

Numbers 23:19

Let us hold unswervingly to the hope we profess, for he who promised is faithful.

Hebrews 10:23

If we are faithless, he will remain faithful, for he cannot disown himself.

2 Timothy 2:13

The LORD is not slow in keeping his promise, as some understand slowness. He is patient with you. . . .

2 Peter 3:9

"Praise be to the LORD, who has given rest to his people Israel just as he promised. Not one word has failed of all the good promises he gave. . . ."

1 Kings 8:56

O LORD, you are my God; I will exalt you and praise your name, for in perfect faithfulness you have done marvelous things, things planned long ago.

Isaiah 25:1

Those who know your name will trust in you, for you, LORD, have never forsaken those who seek you.

Psalms 9:10

All your words are true; all your righteous laws are eternal.

Psalms 119:160

Your word, O LORD, is eternal; it stands firm in the heavens.

Your faithfulness continues through all generations. . . .

Psalms 119:89, 90

"He who is the Glory of Israel does not lie or change his mind; for he is not a man, that he should change his mind."

1 Samuel 15:29

For no matter how many promises God has made, they are "Yes" in Christ. And so through him the 'Amen' is spoken by us to the glory of God.

2 Corinthians 1:20

I will not violate my covenant or alter what my lips have uttered.

Psalms 89:34

"Though the mountains be shaken and the hills be removed, yet my unfailing love for you will not be shaken nor my covenant of peace be removed," says the LORD, who has compassion on you.

Isaiah 54:10

. . . What I have said, that will I bring about; what I have planned, that will I do.

Isaiah 46:11

Fear

He said to his disciples, "Why are you so afraid? Do you still have no faith?"

Mark 4:40

"Do not be afraid, little flock, for your Father had been pleased to give you the kingdom."

Luke 12:32

For I am the LORD, your God, who takes hold of your right hand and says to you, Do not fear; I will help you.

Isaiah 41:13

"But whoever listens to me will live in safety and be at ease, without fear of harm."

Proverbs 1:33

Do not be afraid of those who kill the body but cannot kill the soul. . . .

Matthew 10:28

Have no fear of sudden disaster or of the ruin that overtakes the wicked, for the LORD will be your confidence and will keep your foot from being snared.

Proverbs 3:25, 26

For God did not give us a spirit of timidity, but a spirit of power, of love and of self-discipline.

2 Timothy 1:7

On the day the LORD gives you relief from suffering and turmoil and cruel bondage.

Isaiah 14:3

When you lie down, you will not be afraid; when you lie down, your sleep will be sweet.

Proverbs 3:24

"For the eyes of the LORD are on the righteous and his ears are attentive to their prayer, but the face of the LORD is against those who do evil."

Who is going to harm you if you are eager to do good? But even if you should suffer for what is right, you are blessed. "Do not fear what they fear; do not be frightened."

1 Peter 3:12-14

In righteousness you will be established:

Tyranny will be far from you; you will have nothing to fear.

Terror will be far removed; it will not come near you.

Isaiah 54:14

For you did not receive a spirit that makes you a slave again to fear, but you received the Spirit of sonship. And by him we cry, "*Abba*, Father."

Romans 8:15

So we say with confidence, "The LORD is my helper; I will not be afraid. What can man do to me?"

Hebrews 13:6

God is our refuge and strength, an ever present help in trouble.

Psalms 46:1

"I, even I, am he who comforts you. Who are you that you fear mortal men, the sons of men, who are but grass."

Isaiah 51:12

Fear of man will prove to be a snare, but whoever trusts in the LORD is kept safe.

Proverbs 29:25

He will cover you with his feathers, and under his wings you will find refuge; his faithfulness will be your shield and rampart.

You will not fear the terror of night, nor the arrow that flies by day,

nor the pestilence that stalks in the darkness, nor the plague that destroys at midday.

Psalms 91:4-6

"Do not be afraid; you will not suffer shame.

Do not fear disgrace; you will not be humiliated. . . ."

Isaiah 54:4

When you pass through the waters, I will be with you; and when you pass through the rivers, they will not sweep over you.

When you walk through the fire, you will not be burned; the flames will not set you ablaze.

Isaiah 43:2

Peace I leave with you; my peace I give you. I do not give to you as the world gives. Do not let your hearts be troubled and do not be afraid.

John 14:27

Even though I walk through the valley of the shadow of death, I will fear no evil, for you are with me; your rod and your staff, they comfort me.

You prepare a table before me in the presence of my enemies.

You anoint my head with oil; my cup overflows.

Psalms 23:4, 5

The LORD is my light and my salvation — whom shall I fear?

The LORD is the stronghold of my life — of whom shall I be afraid? . . . Though an army besiege me, my heart will not fear; though war break out against me, even then will I be confident.

Psalms 27:1, 3

No, in all these things we are more than conquerors through him who loved us. For I am convinced that neither death nor life, neither angels nor demons, neither the present nor the future, nor any powers, neither height nor depth, nor anything else in all creation, will be able to separate us from the love of God that is in Christ Jesus our LORD.

Romans 8:37-39

Food and Clothing

You will have plenty to eat, until you are full, and you will praise the name of the LORD your God, who has worked wonders for you; never again will my people be shamed.

Joel 2:26

He grants peace to your borders and satisfies you with the finest of wheat.

Psalms 147:14

He provides food for those who fear him; he remembers his covenant forever.

Psalms 111:5

The righteous eat to their hearts' content, but the stomach of the wicked goes hungry.

Proverbs 13:25

I will bless her with abundant provisions; her poor will I satisfy with food.

Psalms 132:15

So do not worry, saying, "What shall we eat?" or "What shall we drink?" or "What shall we wear?" For the pagans run after all these things, and your heavenly Father knows that you need them.

Matthew 6:31, 32

Forgiveness

But I tell you: Love your enemies and pray for those who persecute you, that you may be sons of your Father in heaven. He causes his sun to rise on the evil and the good, and sends rain on the righteous and the unrighteous.

Matthew 5:44, 45

And when you stand praying, if you hold anything against anyone, forgive him, so that your Father in heaven may forgive you your sins.

Mark 11:25

For if you forgive men when they sin against you, your heavenly Father will also forgive you.

Matthew 6:14

On the contrary: "If your enemy is hungry, feed him; if he is thirsty, give him something to drink. . . ."

Romans 12:20

But love your enemies, do good to them, and lend to them without expecting to get anything back. Then your reward will be great, and you will be sons of the Most High, because he is kind to the ungrateful and wicked. Be merciful, just as your Father is merciful.

"Do not judge, and you will not be judged. Do not condemn, and you will not be condemned. Forgive, and you will be forgiven.

Give, and it will be given to you. A good measure, pressed down, shaken together and running over, will be poured into your lap. For with the measure you use, it will be measured to you."

Luke 6:35-38

Do not say, "I'll pay you back for this wrong!" Wait for the LORD, and he will deliver you.

Proverbs 20:22

Fruitfulness

"I am the true vine, and my Father is the gardener. He cuts off every branch in me that bears no fruit, while every branch that does bear fruit he prunes so that it will be even more fruitful.

You are already clean because of the word I have spoken to you.

Remain in me, and I will remain in you. No branch can bear fruit by itself; it must remain in the vine. Neither can you bear fruit unless you remain in me.

"I am the vine; you are the branches. If a man remains in me and I in him, he will bear much fruit; apart from me you can do nothing."

John 15:1-5

He is like a tree planted by streams of water, which yields its fruit in season and whose leaf does not wither. Whatever he does prospers.

Psalms 1:3

They will come and shout for joy on the heights of Zion; they will rejoice in the bounty of the LORD — the grain, the new wine and the oil, the young of the flocks and herds.

They will be like a well-watered garden, and they will sorrow no more.

Jeremiah 31:12

They will still bear fruit in old age, they will stay fresh and green,

Psalms 92:14

I will be like the dew to Israel; he will blossom like a lily.

Like a cedar of Lebanon he will send down his roots.

Hosea 14:5

For if you possess these qualities in increasing measure, they will keep you from being ineffective and unproductive in your knowledge of our Lord Jesus Christ.

2 Peter 1:8

Gossip

" 'Do not go about spreading slander among your people.
" 'Do not do anything that endangers your neighbor's life. I am the LORD .' "

Leviticus 19:16

The words of a gossip are like choice morsels; they go down to a man's inmost parts.

Proverbs 18:8

A gossip betrays a confidence; so avoid a man who talks too much.

Proverbs 20:19

A gossip betrays a confidence, but a trustworthy man keeps a secret.

Proverbs 11:13

A perverse man stirs up dissension, and a gossip separates close friends.

Proverbs 16:28

Your tongue plots destruction; it is like a sharpened razor, you who practice deceit.

Psalms 52:2

As a north wind brings rain, so a sly tongue brings angry looks.

Proverbs 25:23

Keep your tongue from evil and your lips from speaking lies.

Psalms 34:13

Without wood a fire goes out; without gossip a quarrel dies down.

As charcoal to embers and as wood to fire, so is a quarrelsome man for kindling strife.

Proverbs 26:20-22

Grace, Growth In

This is to my Father's glory, that you bear much fruit, showing yourselves to be my disciples.

John 15:8

And this is my prayer: that your love may abound more and more in knowledge and depth of insight.

Philippians 1:9

We ought always to thank God for you, brothers, and rightly so, because your faith is growing more and more, and the love every one of you has for each other is increasing.

2 Thessalonians 1:3

Finally, brothers, we instructed you how to live in order to please God, as in fact you are living. Now we ask you and urge you in the LORD Jesus to do this more and more.

1 Thessalonians 4:1

Filled with the fruit of righteousness that comes through Jesus Christ — to the glory and praise of God.

Philippians 1:11

For this very reason, make every effort to add to your faith goodness; and to goodness, knowledge.

2 Peter 1:5

Nevertheless, the righteous will hold to their ways, and those with clean hands will grow stronger.

Job 17:9

And we, who with unveiled faces all reflect the LORD'S glory, are being transformed into his likeness with ever-increasing glory, which comes from the LORD, who is the Spirit.

2 Corinthians 3:18

The LORD will fulfill his purpose for me; your love, O LORD, endures forever — do not abandon the works of your hands.

Psalms 138:8

All over the world this gospel is producing fruit and growing, just as it has been doing among you since the day you heard it and understood God's grace in all its truth.

Colossians 1:6

I press on toward the goal to win the prize for which God has called me heavenward in Christ Jesus.

All of us who are mature should take such a view of things. And if on some point you think differently, that too God will make clear to you. Only let us live up to what we have already attained.

Philippians 3:14-16

The path of the righteous is like the first gleam of dawn, shining ever brighter until the full light of day.

Proverbs 4:18

Guidance

Whether you turn to the right or to the left, your ears will hear a voice behind you, saying, "This is the way; walk in it."

Isaiah 30:21

For this God is our God for ever and ever; he will be our guide even to the end.

Psalms 48:14

In his heart a man plans his course, but the LORD determines his steps.

Proverbs 16:9

The LORD delights in the way of the man whose steps he has made firm.

Psalms 37:23

His God instructs him and teaches him the right way.

Isaiah 28:26

The righteousness of the blameless makes a straight way for them, but the wicked are brought down by their own wickedness.

Proverbs 11:5

In all your ways acknowledge him, and he will make your paths straight.

Proverbs 3:6

I will instruct you and teach you in the way you should go; I will counsel you and watch over you.

Psalms 32:8

I will lead the blind by ways they have not known, along unfamiliar paths I will guide them; I will turn the darkness into light before them and make the rough places smooth. These are the things I will do; I will not forsake them.

Isaiah 42:16

Yet I am always with you; you hold me by my right hand.

You guide me with your counsel, and afterward you will take me into glory.

Psalms 73:23, 24

Guilt

If we confess our sins, he is faithful and just and will forgive us our sins and purify us from all unrighteousness.

1 John 1:9

Let the wicked forsake his way and the evil man his thoughts.

Let him turn to the LORD, and he will have mercy on him, and to our God, for he will freely pardon.

Isaiah 55:7

"If you return to the LORD, then your brothers and your children will be shown compassion by their captors and will come back to this land, for the LORD your God is gracious and compassionate. He will not turn his face from you if you return to him."

2 Chronicles 30:9

As far as the east is from the west, so far has he removed our transgressions from us.

Psalms 103:12

Whenever our hearts condemn us. For God is greater than our hearts, and he knows everything.

1 John 3:20

"For I will forgive their wickedness and will remember their sins no more."

Hebrews 8:12

Therefore, if anyone is in Christ, he is a new creation; the old has gone, the new has come!

2 Corinthians 5:17

". . . For I will forgive their wickedness and will re-member their sins no more."

Jeremiah 31:34

I will cleanse them from all the sin they have committed against me and will forgive all their sins of rebellion against me.

Jeremiah 33:8

I write to you, dear children, because your sins have been forgiven on account of his name.

1 John 2:12

"I, even I, am he who blots out your transgressions, for my own sake, and remembers your sins no more."

Isaiah 43:25

But if we walk in the light, as he is in the light, we have fellowship with one another, and the blood of Jesus, his Son, purifies us from all sin.

1 John 1:7

Help in Troubles

The salvation of the righteous comes from the LORD; he is their stronghold in time of trouble.

Psalms 37:39

The LORD gives sight to the blind, the LORD lifts up those who are bowed down, the LORD loves the righteous.

Psalms 146:8

The LORD is good, a refuge in times of trouble.
He cares for those who trust in him.

Nahum 1:7

Though he stumble, he will not fall, for the LORD upholds him with his hand.

Psalms 37:24

You are my hiding place; you will protect me from trouble and surround me with songs of deliverance.

Selah
Psalms 32:7

Though you have made me see troubles, many and bitter, you will restore my life again; from the depths of the earth you will again bring me up.

Psalms 71:20

Why are you downcast, O my soul? Why so disturbed within me?
Put your hope in God, for I will yet praise him, my Saviour and my God.

Psalms 42:11

My flesh and my heart may fail, but God is the strength of my heart and my portion forever.

Psalms 73:26

Then no harm will befall you, no disaster will come near your tent.

For he will command his angels concerning you to guard you in all your ways.

Psalms 91:10, 11

Those who sow in tears will reap with songs of joy.

He who goes out weeping, carrying seed to sow, will return with songs of joy, carrying sheaves with him.

Psalms 126:5, 6

Love the LORD, all his saints! The LORD preserves the faithful, but the proud he pays back in full.

Psalms 31:23

"Even while you sleep among the campfires, the wings of my dove are sheathed with silver, its feathers with shining gold."

Psalms 68:13

"Surely God does not reject a blameless man or strengthen the hands of evildoers.

He will yet fill your mouth with laughter and your lips with shouts of joy."

Job 8:20, 21

From six calamities he will rescue you; in seven no harm will befall you.

Job 5:19

For he has not despised or disdained the suffering of the afflicted one; he has not hidden his face from him but has listened to his cry for help.

Psalms 22:24

The LORD is a refuge for the oppressed, a stronghold in times of trouble.

Psalms 9:9

Though I walk in the midst of trouble, you preserve my life; you stretch out your hand against the anger of my foes, with your right hand you save me.

Psalms 138:7

You, O LORD, keep my lamp burning; my God turns my darkness into light.

Psalms 18:28

A righteous man may have many troubles, but the LORD delivers him from them all.

Psalms 34:19

For men are not cast off by the LORD forever.

Though he brings grief, he will show compassion, so great is his unfailing love.

For he does not willingly bring affliction or grief to the children of men.

Lamentations 3:31-33

The LORD is my rock, my fortress and my deliverer; my God is my rock, in whom I take refuge.

He is my shield and the horn of my salvation, my stronghold.

Psalms 18:2

Do not gloat over me, my enemy!

Though I have fallen, I will rise.

Though I sit in darkness, the LORD will be my light.

Because I have sinned against him, I will bear the LORD'S wrath, until he pleads my case and establishes my right.

He will bring me out into the light; I will see his righteousness.

Micah 7:8, 9

"I have told you these things, so that in me you may have peace. In this world you will have trouble. But take heart! I have overcome the world."

John 16:33

Holy Spirit

... I would have poured out my heart to you and made my thoughts known to you.

Proverbs 1:23

And I will ask the Father, and he will give you another Counselor to be with you forever — the Spirit of truth. The world cannot accept him, because it neither sees him nor knows him. But you know him, for he lives with you and will be in you.

John 14:16, 17

Whoever believes in me, as the Scripture has said, streams of living water will flow from within him."

By this he meant the Spirit, whom those who believed in him were later to receive. Up to that time the Spirit had not been given, since Jesus had not yet been glorified.

John 7:38, 39

But when he, the Spirit of truth, comes, he will guide you into all truth. He will not speak on his own; he will speak only what he hears, and he will tell you what is yet to come.

John 16:13

"As for me, this is my covenant with them," says the LORD. "My Spirit, who is on you, and my words that I have put in your mouth will not depart from your mouth, or from the mouths of your children, or from the mouths of their descendants from this time on and forever," says the LORD.

Isaiah 59:21

"If you then, though you are evil, know how to give good gifts to your children, how much more will your Father in heaven give the Holy Spirit to those who ask him!"

Luke 11:13

"But whoever drinks the water I give him will never thirst. Indeed, the water I give him will become in him a spring of water welling up to eternal life."

John 4:14

And I will put my Spirit in you and move you to follow my decrees and be careful to keep my laws.

Ezekiel 36:27

He redeemed us in order that the blessing given to Abraham might come to the Gentiles through Christ Jesus, so that by faith we might receive the promise of the Spirit.

Galatians 3:14

As for you, the anointing you received from him remains in you, and you do not need anyone to teach you. But as his anointing teaches you about all things and as that anointing is real, not counterfeit — just as it has taught you, remain in him.

1 John 2:27

For the kingdom of God is not a matter of eating and drinking, but of righteousness, peace and joy in the Holy Spirit.

Romans 14:17

In the same way, the Spirit helps us in our weakness. We do not know what we ought to pray but the Spirit himself intercedes for us with groans that words cannot express. And he who searches our hearts knows the mind of the Spirit, because the Spirit intercedes for the saints in accordance with God's will.

Romans 8:26, 27

We have not received the spirit of the world but the Spirit who is from God, that we may understand what God has freely given us.

1 Corinthians 2:12

For you did not receive a spirit that makes you a slave again to fear, but you received the Spirit of sonship. And by him we cry, "*Abba*, Father."

Romans 8:15

Honesty

" 'Do not steal.
" 'Do not lie.
" 'Do not deceive one another.' "

Leviticus 19:11

Am I still to forget, O wicked house, your ill-gotten treasures and the short ephah, which is accursed?

Shall I acquit a man with dishonest scales, with a bag of false weights?

Her rich men are violent; her people are liars and their tongues speak deceitfully.

Micah 6:10-12

" 'Do not use dishonest standards when measuring length, weight or quantity.' "

Leviticus 19:35

The LORD abhors dishonest scales, but accurate weights are his delight.

Proverbs 11:1

You must have accurate and honest weights and measures, so that you may live long in the land the LORD your God is giving you. For the LORD your God detests anyone who does these things, anyone who deals dishonestly.

Deuteronomy 25:15, 16

The wicked borrow and do not repay, but the righteous give generously.

Psalms 37:21

And that in this matter no one should wrong his brother or take advantage of him. The LORD will punish men for all such sins, as we have already told you and warned you. For God did not call us to be impure, but to live a holy life.

1 Thessalonians 4:6, 7

Do not lie to each other, since you take taken off your old self with its practices and have put on the new self, which is being renewed in knowledge in the image of its Creator.

Colossians 3:9, 10

Do not withhold good from those who deserve it, when it is in your power to act.

Proverbs 3:27

" 'If you sell land to one of your countrymen or buy any from him, do not take advantage of each other.' "

Leviticus 25:14

Do not take advantage of each other, but fear your God. I am the LORD your God.

Leviticus 25:17

He who walks righteously and speaks what is right, who rejects gain from extortion and keeps his hand from accepting bribes, who stops his ears against plots of murder and shuts his eyes against contemplating evil — this is the man who will dwell on the heights, whose refuge will be the mountain fortress. His bread will be supplied, and water will not fail him.

Isaiah 33:15, 16

Better a little with righteousness than much gain with injustice.

Proverbs 16:8

Hope

Why are you downcast, O my soul? Why so disturbed within me?

Put your hope in God, for I will yet priase him, my Savior and my God.

Psalms 42:11

Through him you believe in God, who raised him from the dead and glorified him, and so your faith and hope are in God.

1 Peter 1:21

Therefore, prepare your minds for action; be self-controlled; set your hope fully on the grace to be given you when Jesus Christ is revealed.

1 Peter 1:13

Everyone who has this hope in him purifies himself, just as he is pure.

1 John 3:3

When calamity comes, the wicked are brought down, but even in death the righteous have a refuge.

Proverbs 14:32

The faith and love that spring from the hope that is stored up for you in heaven and that you have already heard about in the word of truth, the gospel.

Colossians 1:5

... which is Christ in you, the hope of glory.

Colossians 1:27

Be strong and take heart, all you who hope in the LORD.

Psalms 31:24

For you have been my hope, O Sovereign LORD, my confidence since my youth.

Psalms 71:5

Praise be to the God and Father of our LORD Jesus Christ! In his great mercy he has given us new birth into a living hope through the resurrection of Jesus Christ from the dead.

1 Peter 1:3

Hospitality

Offer hospitality to one another without grumbling.

Each one should use whatever gift he has received to serve others, faithfully administering God's grace in its various forms.

1 Peter 4:9, 10

Suppose a brother or sister is without clothes and daily food. If one of you says to him, "Go, I wish you well; keep warm and well fed," but does nothing about his physical needs, what good is it?

James 2:15, 16

I tell you the truth, anyone who gives you a cup of water in my name because you belong to Christ will certainly not lose his reward.

Mark 9:41

"In everything I did, I showed you that by this kind of hard work we must help the weak, remembering the words the LORD Jesus himself said: 'It is more blessed to give than to receive.' "

Acts 20:35

If anyone has material possessions and sees his brother in need but has no pity on him, how can the love of God be in him?

1 John 3:17

Share with God's people who are in need. Practice hospitality.

Romans 12:13

Our desire is not that others might be relieved while you are hard pressed, but that there might be equality. At the present time your plenty will supply what they need, so that in turn their plenty will supply what you need. Then there will be equality.

2 Corinthians 8:13, 14

" 'For I was hungry and you gave me something to eat, I was thirsty and you gave me something to drink, I was a stranger and you invited me in, I needed clothes and you clothed me, I was sick and you looked after me, I was in prison and you came to visit me.' "

Matthew 25:35, 36

"The King will reply, 'I tell you the truth, whatever you did for one of the least of these brothers of mine, you did for me.' "

Matthew 25:40

Do not forget to entertain strangers, for by so doing some people have entertained angels without knowing it.

Hebrews 13:2

Humility

Therefore, whoever humbles himself like this child is the greatest in the kingdom of heaven.

Matthew 18:4

You hear, O LORD, the desire of the afflicted; you encourage them, and you listen to their cry.

Psalms 10:17

For whoever exalts himself will be humbled, and whoever humbles himself will be exalted.

Matthew 23:12

When men are brought low and you say, "Lift them up!" then he will save the downcast.

Job 22:29

Better to be lowly in spirit and among the oppressed than to share plunder with the proud.

Proverbs 16:19

He mocks proud mockers but gives grace to the humble.

Proverbs 3:34

But he gives us more grace. That is why Scripture says: "God opposes the proud but gives grace to the humble."

James 4:6

For he who avenges blood remembers; he does not ignore the cry of the afflicted.

Psalms 9:12

Humility and the fear of the LORD bring wealth and honor and life.

Proverbs 22:4

The fear of the LORD teaches a man wisdom, and humility comes before honor.

Proverbs 15:33

A man's pride brings him low, but a man of lowly spirit gains honor.

Proverbs 29:23

Humble yourselves, therefore, under God's mighty hand, that he may lift you up in due time.

1 Peter 5:6

Jealousy

"You shall not covet your neighbor's wife. You shall not set your desire on your neighbor's house or land, his manservant or maidservant, his ox or donkey, or anything that belongs to your neighbor."

Deuteronomy 5:21

For where you have envy and selfish ambition, there you find disorder and every evil practice.

James 3:16

Or do you think Scripture says without reason that the spirit he caused to live in us tends toward envy?

James 4:5

Be still before the LORD and wait patiently for him; do not fret when men succeed in their ways, when they carry out their wicked schemes.

Psalms 37:7

He boasts of the cravings of his heart; he blesses the greedy and reviles the LORD.

Psalms 10:3

Do not envy a violent man or choose any of his ways.

Proverbs 3:31

A heart at peace gives life to the body, but envy rots the bones.

Proverbs 14:30

Anger is cruel and fury overwhelming, but who can stand before jealousy?

Proverbs 27:4

And I saw that all labor and all achievement spring from man's envy of his neighbor. This too is meaningless, a chasing after the wind.

Ecclesiastes 4:4

Let us not become conceited, provoking and envying each other.

Galatians 5:26

Do not envy wicked men, do not desire their company.

Proverbs 24:1

But if you harbor bitter envy and selfish ambition in your hearts, do not boast about it or deny the truth.

James 3:14

Do not let your heart envy sinners, but always be zealous for the fear of the LORD.

There is surely a future hope for you, and your hope will not be cut off.

Proverbs 23:17, 18

Then Jesus said to his disciples: "Therefore I tell you, do not worry about your life, what you will eat; or about your body, what you will wear. Life is more than food, and the body more than clothes."

Luke 12:22, 23

Joy

You will go out in joy and be led forth in peace; the mountains and hills will burst into song before you, and all the trees of the field will clap their hands.

Isaiah 55:12

Blessed are those who have learned to acclaim you, who walk in the light of your presence, O LORD.

They rejoice in your name all day long; they exult in your righteousness.

Psalms 89:15, 16

Shouts of joy and victory resound in the tents of the righteous: "The LORD'S right hand has done mighty things!"

Psalms 118:15

You have filled my heart with greater joy than when their grain and new wine abound.

Psalms 4:7

Those who sow in tears will reap with songs of joy.

He who goes out weeping, carrying seed to sow, will return with songs of joy, carrying sheaves with him.

Psalms 126:5, 6

Light is shed upon the righteous and joy on the upright in heart.

Rejoice in the LORD, you who are righteous, and praise his holy name.

Psalms 97:11, 12

Surely then you will find delight in the Almighty and will lift up your face to God.

Job 22:26

I have told you this so that my joy may be in you and that your joy may be complete.

John 15:11

Yet I will rejoice in the LORD, I will be joyful in God my Savior.

Habakkuk 3:18

The ransomed of the LORD will return. They will enter Zion with singing; everlasting joy will crown their heads.

Gladness and joy will overtake them, and sorrow and sighing will flee away.

Isaiah 51:11

In him our hearts rejoice, for we trust in his holy name.

Psalms 33:21

Though you have not seen him, you love him; and even though you do not see him now, you believe in him and are filled with an inexpressible and glorious joy.

1 Peter 1:8

Nehemiah said, "Go and enjoy choice food and sweet drinks, and send some to those who have nothing prepared. This day is sacred to our LORD. Do not grieve, for the joy of the LORD is your strength."

Nehemiah 8:10

I delight greatly in the LORD; my soul rejoices in my God.

For he has clothed me with garments of salvation and arrayed me in a robe of righteousness, as a bridegroom adorns his head like a priest, and as a bride adorns herself with her jewels.

Isaiah 61:10

. . . But you will rejoice in the LORD and glory in the Holy One of Israel.

Isaiah 41:16

Let the righteous rejoice in the LORD and take refuge in him; let all the upright in heart praise him!

Psalms 64:10

My soul will be satisfied as with the richest of foods; with singing lips my mouth will praise you.

Psalms 63:5

But may the righteous be glad and rejoice before God; may they be happy and joyful.

Psalms 68:3

. . . but I will see you again and you will rejoice, and no one will take away your joy.

John 16:22

Laziness

Make it your ambition to lead a quiet life, to mind your own business and to work with your hands, just as we told you, so that your daily life may win the respect of outsiders and so that you will not be dependent on anybody.

1 Thessalonians 4:11, 12

Never be lacking in zeal, but keep your spiritual fervor, serving the LORD.

Romans 12:11

He who works his land will have abundant food, but the one who chases fantasies will have his fill of poverty.

Proverbs 28:19

The sluggard craves and gets nothing, but the desires of the diligent are fully satisfied.

Proverbs 13:4

Lazy hands make a man poor, but diligent hands bring wealth.

He who gathers crops in summer is a wise son, but he who sleeps during harvest is a disgraceful son.

Proverbs 10:4, 5

For even when we were with you, we gave you this rule: "If a man will not work, he shall not eat."

We hear that some among you are idle. They are not busy; they are busybodies. Such people we command and urge in the LORD Jesus Christ to settle down and earn the bread they eat.

2 Thessalonians 3:10-12

A poor man's field may produce abundant food, but injustice sweeps it away.

Proverbs 13:23

The hard-working farmer should be the first to receive a share of the crops.

2 Timothy 2:6

He who has been stealing must steal no longer, but must work, doing something useful with his own hands, that he may have something to share with those in need.

Ephesians 4:28

I went past the field of the sluggard, past the vineyard of the man who lacks judgment;
thorns had come up everywhere, the ground was covered with weeds, and the stone wall was in ruins.
I applied my heart to what I observed and learned a lesson from what I saw:
A little sleep, a little slumber, a little folding of the hands to rest —
and poverty will come on you like a bandit and scarcity like an armed man.

Proverbs 24:30-34

Do not love sleep or you will grow poor; stay awake and you will have food to spare.

Proverbs 20:13

The way of the sluggard is blocked with thorns, but the path of the upright is a highway.

Proverbs 15:19

The plans of the diligent lead to profit as surely as haste leads to poverty.

Proverbs 21:5

Diligent hands will rule, but laziness ends in slave labor.

Proverbs 12:24

He who works his land will have abundant food, but he who chases fantasies lacks judgment.

Proverbs 12:11

Be sure you know the condition of your flocks, give careful attention to your herds.

Proverbs 27:23

You will have plenty of goats' milk to feed you and your family and to nourish your servant girls.

Proverbs 27:27

Then I realized that it is good and proper for a man to eat and drink, and to find satisfaction in his toilsome labor under the sun during the few days of life God has given him — for this is his lot.

Moreover, when God gives any man wealth and possessions, and enables him to enjoy them, to accept his lot and be happy in his work — this is a gift of God.

Ecclesiastes 5:18, 19

Loneliness

I will not leave you as orphans; I will come to you.
John 14:18

Then you will call, and the LORD will answer; you will cry for help, and he will say: Here am I.
Isaiah 58:9

Since you are precious and honored in my sight, and because I love you. . . .
Isaiah 43:4

"I will be a Father to you, and you will be my sons and daughters, says the LORD Almighty."
2 Corinthians 6:18

"I am with you and will watch over you wherever you go, and I will bring you back to this land. I will not leave you until I have done what I have promised you."
Genesis 28:15

And you have been given fullness in Christ, who is the head over every power and authority.
Colossians 2:10

Yet I am poor and needy; may the LORD think of me.
You are my help and my deliverer; O my God, do not delay.
Psalms 40:17

Long Life

Even to your old age and gray hairs I am he, I am he who will sustain you.

I have made you and I will carry you; I will sustain you and I will rescue you.

Isaiah 46:4

Is not wisdom found among the aged? Does not long life bring understanding?

"To God belong wisdom and power; counsel and understanding are his."

Job 12:12, 13

The glory of young men is their strength, gray hair the splendor of the old.

Proverbs 20:29

Children's children are a crown to the aged, and parents are the pride of their children.

Proverbs 17:6

You will come to the grave in full vigor, like sheaves gathered in season.

Job 5:26

Life will be brighter than noonday, and darkness will become like morning.

Job 11:17

Do not cast me away when I am old; do not forsake me when my strength is gone.

Psalms 71:9

You must teach what is in accord with sound doctrine. Teach the older men to be temperate, worthy of respect, self-controlled, and sound in faith, in love and in endurance.

Likewise, teach the older women to be reverent in the way they live, not to be slanderers or addicted to much wine, but to teach what is good. Then they can train the younger women to love their husbands and children, to be self-controlled and pure, to be busy at home, to be kind, and to be subject to their husbands, so that no one will malign the word of God.

Titus 2:1-5

Since my youth, O God, you have taught me, and to this day I declare your marvelous deeds.

Even when I am old and gray, do not forsake me, O God, till I declare your power to the next generation, your might to all who are to come.

Psalms 71:17, 18

Show me, O LORD, my life's end and the number of my days; let me know how fleeting is my life. You have made my days a mere handbreadth; the span of my years is as nothing before you. Each man's life is but a breath. ***Selah***

Psalms 39:4, 5

Walk in all the way that the LORD your God has commanded you, so that you may live and prosper and prolong your days in the land that you will possess.

Deuteronomy 5:33

My son, do not forget my teaching, but keep my commands in your heart, for they will prolong your life many years and bring you prosperity.

Proverbs 3:1, 2

So that you, your children and their children after them may fear the LORD your God as long as you live by keeping all his decrees and commands that I give you, and so that you may enjoy long life.

Deuteronomy 6:2

"With long life will I satisfy him and show him my salvation."

Psalms 91:16

The fear of the LORD adds length to life; but the years of the wicked are cut short.

Proverbs 10:27

For through me your days will be many, and years will be added to your life.

Proverbs 9:11

Love, Brotherly

"A new command I give you: Love one another. As I have loved you, so you must love one another.

All men will know that you are my disciples if you love one another."

John 13:34, 35

Love must be sincere. Hate what is evil; cling to what is good.

Be devoted to one another in brotherly love. Honor one another above yourselves.

Romans 12:9, 10

Now about brotherly love we do not need to write to you, for you yourselves have been taught by God to love each other.

1 Thessalonians 4:9

Whoever loves his brother lives in the light, and there is nothing in him to make him stumble.

1 John 2:10

Now that you have purified yourselves by obeying the truth so that you have sincere love for your brothers, love one another deeply, from the heart.

1 Peter 1:22

Dear friends, let us love one another, for love comes from God. Everyone who loves has been born of God and knows God. Whoever does not love does not know God, because God is love.

1 John 4:7, 8

Dear children, let us not love with words or tongue but with actions and in truth.

1 John 3:18

Dear friends, since God so loved us, we also ought to love one another.

1 John 4:11

Therefore, as God's chosen people, holy and dearly loved, clothe yourselves with compassion, kindness, humility, gentleness and patience. Bear with each other and forgive whatever grievances you may have against one another. Forgive as the LORD forgave you.

Colossians 3:12, 13

Love, God's

For God so loved the world that he gave his one and only Son, that whoever believes in him shall not perish but have eternal life.

John 3:16

He will love you and bless you and increase your numbers. He will bless the fruit of your womb, the crops of your land — your grain, new wine and oil — the calves of your herds and the lambs of your flocks in the land that he swore to your forefathers to give you.

Deuteronomy 7:13

The LORD gives sight to the blind, the LORD lifts up those who are bowed down, the LORD loves the righteous.

Psalms 146:8

The LORD detests the way of the wicked but he loves those who pursue righteousness.

Proverbs 15:9

As a young man marries a maiden, so will your sons marry you; as a bridegroom rejoices over his bride, so will your God rejoice over you.

Isaiah 62:5

The LORD appeared to us in the past, saying: "I have loved you with an everlasting love; I have drawn you with loving-kindness."

Jeremiah 31:3

The LORD your God is with you, he is mighty to save.

He will take great delight in you, he will quiet you with his love, he will rejoice over you with singing."

Zephaniah 3:17

"I will heal their waywardness and love them freely, for my anger has turned away from them."

Hosea 14:4

I will rejoice in doing them good and will assuredly plant them in this land with all my heart and soul.

Jeremiah 32:41

But because of his great love for us, God, who is rich in mercy, made us alive with Christ even when we were dead in transgressions — it is by grace you have been saved.

And God raised us up with Christ and seated us with him in the heavenly realms in Christ Jesus, in order that in the coming ages he might show the incomparable riches of his grace, expressed in his kindness to us in Christ Jesus.

Ephesians 2:4-7

This is love: not that we loved God, but that he loved us and sent his Son as an atoning sacrifice for our sins.

1 John 4:10

No, the Father himself loves you because you have loved me and have believed that I came from God.

John 16:27

And so we know and rely on the love God has for us.

God is love. Whoever lives in love lives in God, and God in him.

1 John 4:16

We love because he first loved us.

1 John 4:19

"I have made you known to them, and will continue to make you known in order that the love you have for me may be in them and that I myself may be in them."

John 17:26

I in them and you in me. May they be brought to complete unity to let the world know that you sent me and have loved them even as you have loved me.

John 17:23

May our LORD Jesus Christ himself and God our Father, who loved us and by his grace gave us eternal encouragement and good hope, encourage your hearts and strengthen you in every good deed and word.

2 Thessalonians 2:16, 17

Loving God

Know therefore that the LORD your God is God; he is the faithful God, keeping his covenant of love to a thousand generations of those who love him and keep his commands.

Deuteronomy 7:9

I love those who love me, and those who seek me find me.

Proverbs 8:17

Whoever has my commands and obeys them, he is the one who loves me. He who loves me will be loved by my Father, and I too will love him and show myself to him."

John 14:21

Bestowing wealth on those who love me and making their treasuries full.

Proverbs 8:21

Delight yourself in the LORD and he will give you the desires of your heart.

Psalms 37:4

The LORD watches over all who love him, but all the wicked he will destroy.

Psalms 145:20

Grace to all who love our LORD Jesus Christ with an undying love.

Ephesians 6:24

"Because he loves me," says the LORD, "I will rescue him; I will protect him, for he acknowledges my name."

Psalms 91:14

However, as it is written: "No eye has seen, no ear has heard, no mind has conceived what God has prepared for those who love him."

1 Corinthians 2:9

So if you faithfully obey the commands I am giving you today — to love the LORD your God and to serve him with all your heart and with all your soul —

then I will rain on your land in its season, both autumn and spring rains, so that you may gather in your grain, new wine and oil.

I will provide grass in the fields for your cattle, and you will eat and be satisfied.

Deuteronomy 11:13-15

Lust

What causes fights and quarrels among you? Don't they come from your desires that battle within you? You want something but don't get it. You kill and covet, but you cannot have what you want. You quarrel and fight. You do not have, because you do not ask God.

When you ask, you do not receive, because you ask with wrong motives, that you may spend what you get on your pleasures.

You adulterous people, don't you know that friendship with the world is hatred toward God? Anyone who chooses to be a friend of the world becomes an enemy of God.

James 4:1-4

For everything in the world — the cravings of sinful man, the lust of his eyes and the boasting of what he has and does — comes not from the Father but from the world. The world and its desires pass away, but the man who does the will of God lives forever.

1 John 2:16, 17

"You have heard that it was said, 'Do not commit adultery.' But I tell you that anyone who looks at a woman lustfully has already committed adultery with her in his heart."

Matthew 5:27, 28

Do not lust in your heart after her beauty or let her captivate you with her eyes,

for the prostitute reduces you to a loaf of bread, and the adulteress preys upon your very life.

Can a man scoop fire into his lap without his clothes being burned?

Can a man walk on hot coals without his feet being scorched?

So is he who sleeps with another man's wife; no one who touches her will go unpunished.

Proverbs 6:25-29

Submit yourselves, then, to God. Resist the devil, and he will flee from you. Come near to God and he will come near to you. Wash your hands, you sinners, and purify your hearts, you double-minded.

James 4:7, 8

Dear friends, I urge you, as aliens and strangers in the world, to abstain from sinful desires, which war against your soul.

1 Peter 2:11

As obedient children, do not conform to the evil desires you had when you lived in ignorance.

But just as he who called you is holy, so be holy in all you do; for it is written: "Be holy, because I am holy."

1 Peter 1:14-16

Flee the evil desires of youth, and pursue righteousness, faith, love and peace, along with those who call on the LORD out of a pure heart.

2 Timothy 2:22

At one time we too were foolish, disobedient, deceived and enslaved by all kinds of passions and pleasures. We lived in malice and envy, being hated and hating one another. But when the kindness and love of God our Savior appeared, he saved us, not because of righteous things we had done, but because of his mercy. He saved us through the washing of rebirth and renewal by the Holy Spirit.

Titus 3:3-5

All of us also lived among them at one time, gratifying the cravings of our sinful nature and following its desires and thoughts. Like the rest, we were by nature objects of wrath. But because of his great love for us, God, who is rich in mercy, made us alive with Christ even when we were dead in transgressions — it is by grace you have been saved.

And God raised us up with Christ and seated us with him in the heavenly realms in Christ Jesus.

Ephesians 2:3-6

For the grace of God that brings salvation has appeared to all men.

It teaches us to say "No" to ungodliness and worldly passions, and to live self-controlled, upright and godly lives in this present age.

Titus 2:11, 12

When tempted, no one should say, "God is tempting me." For God cannot be tempted by evil, nor does he tempt anyone.

James 1:13

Those who belong to Christ Jesus have crucified the sinful nature with its passions and desires.

Galatians 5:24

They said to you, "In the last times there will be scoffers who will follow their own ungodly desires." These are the men who divide you, who follow mere natural instincts and do not have the Spirit.

But you, dear friends, build yourselves up in your most holy faith and pray in the Holy Spirit.

Keep yourselves in God's love as you wait for the mercy of your LORD Jesus Christ to bring you to eternal life.

Jude 18-21

. . . Live by the Spirit, and you will not gratify the desires of the sinful nature. For the sinful nature desires what is contrary to the Spirit, and the Spirit what is contrary to the sinful nature. They are in conflict with each other, so that you do not do what you want.

Galatians 5:16, 17

In the same way, count yourselves dead to sin but alive to God in Christ Jesus. Therefore do not let sin reign in your mortal body so that you obey its evil desires. . . . For sin shall not be your master, because you are not under law, but under grace.

Romans 6:11, 12, 14

Through these he has given us his very great and precious promises, so that through them you may participate in the divine nature and escape the corruption in the world caused by evil desires.

2 Peter 1:4

Lying

Do not lie to each other, since you have taken off your old self with its practices and have put on the new self, which is being renewed in knowledge in the image of its Creator.

Colossians 3:9, 10

" 'Do not swear falsely by my name and so profane the name of your God. I am the LORD.' "

Leviticus 19:12

Like a club or a sword or a sharp arrow is the man who gives false testimony against his neighbor.

Proverbs 25:18

"Do not plot evil against your neighbor, and do not love to swear falsely. I hate all this," declares the LORD.

Zechariah 8:17

A truthful witness does not deceive, but a false witness pours out lies.

Proverbs 14:5

. . . "How many times must I make you swear to tell me nothing but the truth in the name of the LORD?"

1 Kings 22:16

A false witness will not go unpunished, and he who pours out lies will not go free.

Proverbs 19:5

If a malicious witness takes the stand to accuse a man of a crime, the two men involved in the dispute must stand in the presence of the LORD before the priests and the judges who are in office at the time. The judges must make a thorough investigation, and if the witness proves to be a liar, giving false testimony against his brother, then do to him as he intended to do to his brother. You must purge the evil from among you.

Deuteronomy 19:16-19

"But the cowardly, the unbelieving, the vile, the murderers, the sexually immoral, those who practice magic arts, the idolaters and all liars — their place will be in the fiery lake of burning sulfur. This is the second death."

Revelation 21:8

A false witness will not go unpunished, and he who pours out lies will perish.

Proverbs 19:9

Do not testify against your neighbor without cause, or use your lips to deceive.

Proverbs 24:28

Even from birth the wicked go astray; from the womb they are wayward and speak lies.

Psalms 58:3

But if you harbor bitter envy and selfish ambition in your hearts, do not boast about it or deny the truth.

James 3:14

"Do not spread false reports. Do not help a wicked man by being a malicious witness."

Exodus 23:1

Truthful lips endure forever, but a lying tongue lasts only a moment.

Proverbs 12:19

Marriage

Enjoy life with your wife, whom you love, all the days of this meaningless life that God has given you under the sun — all your meaningless days. For this is your lot in life and in your toilsome labor under the sun.

Ecclesiastes 9:9

Drink water from your own cistern, running water from your own well.

Proverbs 5:15

May your fountain be blessed, and may you rejoice in the wife of your youth.

A loving doe, a graceful deer — may her breasts satisfy you always, may you ever be captivated by her love.

Why be captivated, my son, by an adulteress? Why embrace the bosom of another man's wife?

Proverbs 5:18-20

The husband should fulfill his marital duty to his wife, and likewise the wife to her husband.

1 Corinthians 7:3

Wives, submit to your husbands as to the LORD. For the husband is the head of the wife as Christ is the head of the church, his body, of which he is the Savior.

Ephesians 5:22, 23

Husbands, love your wives, just as Christ loved the church and gave himself up for her.

Ephesians 5:25

In this same way, husbands ought to love their wives as their own bodies. He who loves his wife loves himself.

Ephesians 5:28

"For this reason a man will leave his father and mother and be united to his wife, and the two will become one flesh."

Ephesians 5:31

If anyone does not provide for his relatives, and especially for his immediate family, he has denied the faith and is worse than an unbeliever.

1 Timothy 5:8

Wives, submit to your husbands, as is fitting in the LORD.
Husbands, love your wives and do not be harsh with them.

Colossians 3:18, 19

Husbands, in the same way be considerate as you live with your wives, and treat them with respect as the weaker partner and as heirs with you of the gracious gift of life, so that nothing will hinder your prayers.

1 Peter 3:7

Then they can train the younger women to love their husbands and children, to be self-controlled and pure, to be busy at home, to be kind, and to be subject to their husbands, so that no one will malign the word of God.

Titus 2:4, 5

Meekness

Blessed are the meek, for they will inherit the earth.

Matthew 5:5

But with righteousness he will judge the needy, with justice he will give decisions for the poor of the earth. . . .

Isaiah 11:4

The poor will eat and be satisfied; they who seek the LORD will praise him — may your hearts live forever!

Psalms 22:26

For the LORD takes delight in his people; he crowns the humble with salvation.

Psalms 149:4

Once more the humble will rejoice in the LORD; the needy will rejoice in the Holy One of Israel.

Isaiah 29:19

The LORD sustains the humble but casts the wicked to the ground.

Psalms 147:6

He guides the humble in what is right and teaches them his way.

Psalms 25:9

Instead, it should be that of your inner self, the unfading beauty of a gentle and quiet spirit, which is of great worth in God's sight.

1 Peter 3:4

Seek the LORD, all you humble of the land, you who do what he commands.

Seek righteousness, seek humility; perhaps you will be sheltered on the day of the LORD's anger.

Zephaniah 2:3

But the meek will inherit the land and enjoy great peace.

Psalms 37:11

A gentle answer turns away wrath, but a harsh word stirs up anger.

Proverbs 15:1

Mercy

Yet the LORD longs to be gracious to you; he rises to show you compassion.

For the LORD is a God of justice. Blessed are all who wait for him!

Isaiah 30:18

. . . Know this: God has even forgotten some of your sin.

Job 11:6

As a father has compassion on his children, so the LORD has compassion on those who fear him.

Psalms 103:13

But from everlasting to everlasting the LORD'S love is with those who fear him, and his righteousness with their children's children.

Psalms 103:17

And the LORD said, "I will cause all my goodness to pass in front of you, and I will proclaim my name, the LORD, in your presence. I will have mercy on whom I will have mercy, and I will have compassion on whom I will have compassion."

Exodus 33:19

". . . I will show my love to the one I called 'Not my loved one.'

I will say to those called 'Not my people,' 'You are my people'; and they will say, 'You are my God.' "

Hosea 2:23

. . . Though in anger I struck you, in favor I will show you compassion.

Isaiah 60:10

For my own name's sake I delay my wrath; for the sake of my praise I hold it back from you, so as not to cut you off.

Isaiah 48:9

Money

Do not wear yourself out to get rich; have the wisdom to show restraint.

Cast but a glance at riches, and they are gone, for they will surely sprout wings and fly off to the sky like an eagle.

Proverbs 23:4, 5

Better the little that the righteous have than the wealth of many wicked.

Psalms 37:16

Listen, my dear brothers: Has not God chosen those who are poor in the eyes of the world to be rich in faith and to inherit the kingdom he promised those who love him?

James 2:5

Better one handful with tranquillity than two handfuls with toil and chasing after the wind.

Ecclesiastes 4:6

"Because of the oppression of the weak and the groaning of the needy, I will now arise," says the LORD. "I will protect them from those who malign them."

Psalms 12:5

He who mocks the poor shows contempt for their Maker; whoever gloats over disaster will not go unpunished.

Proverbs 17:5

Do not exploit the poor because they are poor and do not crush the needy in court.

Proverbs 22:22

Command those who are rich in this present world not to be arrogant nor to put their hope in wealth, which is so uncertain, but to put their hope in God, who richly provides us with everything for our enjoyment. Command them to do good, to be rich in good deeds, and to be generous and willing to share. In this way they will lay up treasure for themselves as a firm foundation for the coming age, so that they may take hold of the life that is truly life.

1 Timothy 6:17-19

The sleep of a laborer is sweet, whether he eats little or much, but the abundance of a rich man permits him no sleep.

I have seen a grievous evil under the sun: wealth hoarded to the harm of its owner, or wealth lost through some misfortune, so that when he has a son there is nothing left for him.

Ecclesiastes 5:12-14

But remember the LORD your God, for it is he who gives you the ability to produce wealth, and so confirms his covenant, which he swore to your forefathers, as it is today.

Deuteronomy 8:18

But the needy will not always be forgotten, nor the hope of the afflicted ever perish.

Psalms 9:18

He saves the needy from the sword in their mouth; he saves them from the clutches of the powerful.

So the poor have hope, and injustice shuts its mouth.

Job 5:15, 16

Whoever trusts in his riches will fall, but the righteous will thrive like a green leaf.

Proverbs 11:28

A faithful man will be richly blessed, but one eager to get rich will not go unpunished.

Proverbs 28:20

Wealth is worthless in the day of wrath, but righteousness delivers from death.

Proverbs 11:4

They will throw their silver into the streets, and their gold will be an unclean thing. Their silver and gold will not be able to save them in the day of the LORD'S wrath. They will not satisfy their hunger or fill their stomachs with it, for it has made them stumble into sin.

Ezekiel 7:19

One man pretends to be rich, yet has nothing; another pretends to be poor, yet has great wealth.

Proverbs 13:7

Whoever loves money never has money enough; whoever loves wealth is never satisfied with his income. This too is meaningless.

Ecclesiastes 5:10

He who oppresses the poor to increase his wealth and he who gives gifts to the rich — both come to poverty.

Proverbs 22:16

A stingy man is eager to get rich and is unaware that poverty awaits him.

Proverbs 28:22

Rich and poor have this in common: The LORD is the Maker of them all.

Proverbs 22:2

But those who suffer he delivers in their suffering; he speaks to them in their affliction.

Job 36:15

Better a little with the fear of the LORD than great wealth with turmoil.

Proverbs 15:16

Better a poor man whose walk is blameless than a rich man whose ways are perverse.

Proverbs 28:6

Blessed is he who has regard for the weak; the LORD delivers him in times of trouble.

Psalms 41:1

Obedience

See, I set before you today life and prosperity, death and destruction. For I command you today to love the LORD your God, to talk in his ways, and to keep his commands, decrees and laws; then you will live and increase, and the LORD your God will bless you in the land you are entering to possess.

Deuteronomy 30:15, 16

Do what is right and good in the LORD'S sight, so that it may go well with you and you may go in and take over the good land that the LORD promised on oath to your forefathers, thrusting out all your enemies before you, as the LORD said.

Deuteronomy 6:18

Hear, O Israel, and be careful to obey so that it may go well with you and that you may increase greatly in a land flowing with milk and honey, just as the LORD, the God of your fathers, promised you.

Deuteronomy 6:3

If you pay attention to these laws and are careful to follow them, then the LORD your God will keep his covenant of love with you, as he swore to your forefathers.

Deuteronomy 7:12

Oh, that their hearts would be inclined to fear me and keep all my commands always, so that it might go well with them and their children forever!

Deuteronomy 5:29

Carefully follow the terms of this covenant, so that you may prosper in everything you do.

Deuteronomy 29:9

Whatever you have learned or received or heard from me, or seen in me — put it into practice. And the God of peace will be with you.

Philippians 4:9

Anyone who breaks one of the least of these commandments and teaches others to do the same will be called least in the kingdom of heaven, but whoever practices and teaches these commands will be called great in the kingdom of heaven.

Matthew 5:19

"Therefore everyone who hears these words of mine and puts them into practice is like a wise man who built his house on the rock. The rain came down, the streams rose, and the winds blew and beat against that house; yet it did not fall, because it had its foundation on the rock."

Matthew 7:24, 25

If they obey and serve him, they will spend the rest of their days in prosperity and their years in contentment.

Job 36:11

And we know that in all things God works for the good of those who love him, who have been called according to his purpose.

Romans 8:28

If you obey my commands, you will remain in my love, just as I have obeyed my Father's commands and remain in his love.

John 15:10

Now that you know these things, you will be blessed if you do them.

John 13:17

But the man who looks intently into the perfect law that gives freedom, and continues to do this, not forgetting what he has heard, but doing it — he will be blessed in what he does.

James 1:25

And receive from him anything we ask, because we obey his commands and do what pleases him.

1 John 3:22

For it is not those who hear the law who are righteous in God's sight, but it is those who obey the law who will be declared righteous.

Romans 2:13

"I tell you the truth, whoever hears my word and believes him who sent me has eternal life and will not be condemned; he has crossed over from death to life."

John 5:24

"For whoever does the will of my Father in heaven is my brother and sister and mother."

Matthew 12:50

The world and its desires pass away, but the man who does the will of God lives forever.

1 John 2:17

"Not everyone who says to me, 'LORD, LORD,' will enter the kingdom of heaven, but only he who does the will of my Father who is in heaven."

Matthew 7:21

Blessed are they who maintain justice, who constantly do what is right.

Psalms 106:3

And, once made perfect, he became the source of eternal salvation for all who obey him.

Hebrews 5:9

"I tell you the truth, if anyone keeps my word, he will never see death."

John 8:51

Parents' Duties

For I have chosen him, so that he will direct his children and his household after him to keep the way of the LORD by doing what is right and just. . . .

Genesis 18:19

. . . we will tell the next generation the praise-worthy deeds of the LORD, his power, and the wonders he has done.

He decreed statutes for Jacob and established the law in Israel, which he commanded our forefathers to teach their children,

so the next generation would know them, even the children yet to be born, and they in turn would tell their children.

Then they would put their trust in God and would not forget his deeds but would keep his commands.

Psalms 78:4-7

Teach them to your children, talking about them when you sit at home and when you walk along the road, when you lie down and when you get up.

Deuteronomy 11:19

"On that day tell your son, 'I do this because of what the LORD did for me when I came out of Egypt.' "

Exodus 13:8

Train a child in the way he should go, and when he is old he will not turn from it.

Proverbs 22:6

Only be careful, and watch yourselves closely so that you do not forget the things your eyes have seen or let them slip from your heart as long as you live. Teach them to your children and to their children after them. . . . "Assemble the people before me to hear my words so that they may learn to revere me as long as they live in the land and may teach them to their children."

Deuteronomy 4:9, 10

Discipline your son, and he will give you peace; he will bring delight to your soul.

Proverbs 29:17

Fathers, do not exasperate your children; instead, bring them up in the training and instruction of the LORD.

Ephesians 6:4

Fathers, do not embitter your children, or they will become discouraged.

Colossians 3:21

Patience

Be patient, then, brothers, until the LORD'S coming. See how the farmer waits for the land to yield its valuable crop and how patient he is for the autumn and spring rains.

You too, be patient and stand firm, because the LORD'S coming is near.

James 5:7, 8

But how is it to your credit if you receive a beating for doing wrong and endure it? But if you suffer for doing good and you endure it, this is commendable before God.

1 Peter 2:20

Let us not become weary in doing good, for at the proper time we will reap a harvest if we do not give up.

Galatians 6:9

Let us hold unswervingly to the hope we profess, for he who promised is faithful.

Hebrews 10:23

But he who stands firm to the end will be saved.

Matthew 24:13

We do not want you to become lazy, but to imitate those who through faith and patience inherit what has been promised.

Hebrews 6:12

You need to persevere so that when you have done the will of God, you will receive what he has promised.

Hebrews 10:36

Consider it pure joy, my brothers, whenever you face trials of many kinds, because you know that the testing of your faith develops perseverance. Perseverance must finish its work so that you may be mature and complete, not lacking anything.

James 1:2-4

Not only so, but we also rejoice in our sufferings, because we know that suffering produces perseverance; perseverance, character; and character, hope.

Romans 5:3, 4

Peace

". . . Peace, peace, to those far and near," says the LORD. "And I will heal them."

Isaiah 57:19

Let the peace of Christ rule in your hearts, since as members of one body you were called to peace. And be thankful.

Colossians 3:15

I will listen to what God the LORD will say; he promises peace to his people, his saints. . . .

Psalms 85:8

And the peace of God, which transcends all understanding, will guard your hearts and your minds in Christ Jesus.

Philippians 4:7

The fruit of righteousness will be peace; the effect of righteousness will be quietness and confidence forever.

Isaiah 32:17

. . . "Your faith has saved you; go in peace."

Luke 7:50

Consider the blameless, observe the upright; there is a future for the man of peace.

Psalms 37:37

Now may the LORD of peace himself give you peace at all times and in every way. . . .

2 Thessalonians 3:16

Peace I leave with you; my peace I give you. I do not give to you as the world gives. Do not let your hearts be troubled and do not be afraid.

John 14:27

Poverty

For he will deliver the needy who cry out, the afflicted who have no one to help.

He will take pity on the weak and the needy and save the needy from death.

Psalms 72:12, 13

But he lifted the needy out of their affliction and increased their families like flocks.

Psalms 107:41

The LORD hears the needy and does not despise his captive people.

Psalms 69:33

Sing to the LORD! Give praise to the LORD! He rescues the life of the needy from the hands of the wicked.

Jeremiah 20:13

He will respond to the prayer of the destitute; he will not despise their plea.

Psalms 102:17

He raises the poor from the dust and lifts the needy from the ash heap.

Psalms 113:7

I will bless her with abundant provisions; her poor will I satisfy with food.

Psalms 132:15

. . . O God, you provided for the poor.

Psalms 68:10

Prayer

"Ask and it will be given to you; seek and you will find; knock and the door will be opened to you.

For everyone who asks receives; he who seeks finds; and to him who knocks, the door will be opened."

Matthew 7:7, 8

"If you believe, you will receive whatever you ask for in prayer."

Matthew 21:22

. . . How gracious he will be when you cry for help! As soon as he hears, he will answer you.

Isaiah 30:19

This is the assurance we have in approaching God: that if we ask anything according to his will, he hears us.

And if we know that he hears us — whatever we ask — we know that we have what we asked of him.

1 John 5:14, 15

Then you will call upon me and come and pray to me, and I will listen to you.

Jeremiah 29:12

Before they call I will answer; while they are still speaking I will hear.

Isaiah 65:24

You will pray to him, and he will hear you. . . .

Job 22:27

. . . My Father will give you whatever you ask in my name. Until now you have not asked for anything in my name. Ask and you will receive, and your joy will be complete.

John 16:23, 24

Therefore confess your sins to each other and pray for each other so that you may be healed. The prayer of a righteous man is powerful and effective.

James 5:16

And I will do whatever you ask in my name, so that the Son will bring glory to the Father.

You may ask me for anything in my name, and I will do it.

John 14:13, 14

If you remain in me and my words remain in you, ask whatever you wish, and it will be given you.

John 15:7

When you pray, go into your room, close the door and pray to your Father, who is unseen. Then your Father, who sees what is done in secret, will reward you.

Matthew 6:6

And call upon me in the day of trouble; I will deliver you, and you will honor me.

Psalms 50:15

Then you will call, and the LORD will answer; you will cry for help, and he will say: Here am I. . . .

Isaiah 58:9

The Lord is far from the wicked but he hears the prayer of the righteous.

Proverbs 15:29

He will call upon me, and I will answer him. . . .

Psalms 91:15

O you who hear prayer, to you all men will come.

Psalms 65:2

If you, then, though you are evil, know how to give good gifts to your children, how much more will your Father in heaven give good gifts to those who ask him!

Matthew 7:11

The righteous cry out, and the Lord hears them; he delivers them from all their troubles.

Psalms 34:17

Evening, morning and noon I cry out in distress, and he hears my voice.

Psalms 55:17

The Lord is near to all who call on him, to all who call on him in truth.

He fulfills the desires of those who fear him; he hears their cry and saves them.

Psalms 145:18, 19

Do not be like them, for your Father knows what you need before you ask him.

Matthew 6:8

And receive from him anything we ask, because we obey his commands and do what pleases him.

1 John 3:22

"This third I will bring into the fire; I will refine them like silver and test them like gold.

They will call on my name and I will answer them; I will say, 'They are my people,' and they will say, 'The LORD is our God.' "

Zechariah 13:9

"Call to me and I will answer you and tell you great and unsearchable things you do not know."

Jeremiah 33:3

Therefore I tell you, whatever you ask for in prayer, believe that you have received it, and it will be yours.

Mark 11:24

Pride

Pride goes before destruction, a haughty spirit before a fall.

Proverbs 16:18

Woe to those who are wise in their own eyes and clever in their own sight.

Isaiah 5:21

Do you see a man wise in his own eyes? There is more hope for a fool than for him.

Proverbs 26:12

Look at every proud man and humble him, crush the wicked where they stand.

Job 40:12

Haughty eyes and a proud heart, the lamp of the wicked, are sin!

Proverbs 21:4

You rebuke the arrogant, who are cursed and who stray from your commands.

Psalms 119:21

A greedy man stirs up dissension, but he who trusts in the LORD will prosper.

He who trusts in himself is a fool, but he who walks in wisdom is kept safe.

Proverbs 28:25, 26

To fear the LORD is to hate evil; I hate pride and arrogance, evil behavior and perverse speech.

Proverbs 8:13

He said to them, "You are the ones who justify yourselves in the eyes of men, but God knows your hearts. What is highly valued among men is detestable in God's sight."

Luke 16:15

Let another praise you, and not your own mouth; someone else, and not your own lips.

Proverbs 27:2

But, "Let him who boasts boast in the LORD."
For it is not the man who commends himself who is approved, but the man whom the LORD commends.

2 Corinthians 10:17, 18

How can you believe if you accept praise from one another, yet make no effort to obtain the praise that comes from the only God?

John 5:44

Sitting down, Jesus called the Twelve and said, "If anyone wants to be first, he must be the very last, and the servant of all."

Mark 9:35

Prisoners

But this is what the LORD says: "Yes, captives will be taken from warriors, and plunder retrieved from the fierce; I will contend with those who contend with you, and your children I will save."

Isaiah 49:25

Even if you have been banished to the most distant land under the heavens, from there the LORD your God will gather you and bring you back.

Deuteronomy 30:4

The LORD hears the needy and does not despise his captive people.

Psalms 69:33

He brought them out of darkness and the deepest gloom and broke away their chains.

Psalms 107:14

He upholds the cause of the oppressed and gives food to the hungry.
The LORD sets prisoners free.

Psalms 146:7

God sets the lonely in families, he leads forth the prisoners with singing; but the rebellious live in a sunscorched land.

Psalms 68:6

Protection, God's

The name of the LORD is a strong tower; the right-eous run to it and are safe.

Proverbs 18:10

You will laugh at destruction and famine, and need not fear the beasts of the earth.

Job 5:22

You will be secure, because there is hope; you will look about you and take your rest in safety.

You will lie down, with no one to make you afraid, and many will court your favor.

Job 11:18, 19

The LORD will keep you from all harm — he will watch over your life;

the LORD will watch over your coming and going both now and forevermore.

Psalms 121:7, 8

When you lie down, you will not be afraid; when you lie down, your sleep will be sweet.

Proverbs 3:24

Who is going to harm you if you are eager to do good?

1 Peter 3:13

. . . "Let the beloved of the LORD rest secure in him, for he shields him all day long, and the one the LORD loves rests between his shoulders."

Deuteronomy 33:12

He will have no fear of bad news; his heart is steadfast, trusting in the LORD.

Psalms 112:7

If you make the Most High your dwelling — even the LORD, who is my refuge —
Then no harm will befall you, no disaster will come near your tent.

Psalms 91:9, 10

But now, this is what the LORD says — he who created you, O Jacob, he who formed you, O Israel: "Fear not, for I have redeemed you; I have summoned you by name; you are mine.

When you pass through the waters, I will be with you; and when you pass through the rivers, they will not sweep over you.

When you walk through the fire, you will not be burned; the flames will not set you ablaze.

Isaiah 43:1, 2

They will no longer be plundered by the nations, nor will wild animals devour them. They will live in safety, and no one will make them afraid.

Ezekiel 34:28

"But whoever listens to me will live in safety and be at ease, without fear of harm."

Proverbs 1:33

I will lie down and sleep in peace, for you alone, O LORD, make me dwell in safety.

Psalms 4:8

The LORD is my light and my salvation — whom shall I fear?

Psalms 27:1

Repentance

"The time has come," he said. "The kingdom of God is near. Repent and believe the good news!"

Mark 1:15

They went out and preached that people should repent.

Mark 6:12

The LORD is close to the brokenhearted and saves those who are crushed in spirit.

Psalms 34:18

He heals the brokenhearted and binds up their wounds.

Psalms 147:3

If you put away the sin that is in your hand and allow no evil to dwell in your tent,
then you will lift up your face without shame; you will stand firm and without fear.

Job 11:14, 15

"But if a wicked man turns away from all the sins he has committed and keeps all my decrees and does what is just and right, he will surely live; he will not die.
None of the offenses he has committed will be remembered against him. Because of the righteous things he has done, he will live."

Ezekiel 18:21, 22

Righteousness

For the LORD God is a sun and shield; the LORD bestows favor and honor.

Psalms 84:11

The lions may grow weak and hungry, but those who seek the LORD lack no good thing.

Psalms 34:10

What the wicked dreads will overtake him; what the righteous desire will be granted.

Proverbs 10:24

Misfortune pursues the sinner, but prosperity is the reward of the righteous.

Proverbs 13:21

A good man obtains favor from the LORD, but the LORD condemns a crafty man.

Proverbs 12:2

But seek first his kingdom and his righteousness, and all these things will be given to you as well.

Matthew 6:33

Whoever trusts in his riches will fall, but the righteous will thrive like a green leaf.

Proverbs 11:28

Then men will say, "Surely the righteous still are rewarded. . . ."

Psalms 58:11

For surely, O LORD, you bless the righteous; you surround them with your favor as with a shield.

Psalms 5:12

From the LORD comes deliverance. May your blessing be on your people. *Selah*

Psalms 3:8

Whether Paul or Apollos or Cephas or the world or life or death or the present or the future — all are yours, and you are of Christ, and Christ is of God.

1 Corinthians 3:22, 23

He who did not spare his own Son, but gave him up for us all — how will he not also, along with him, graciously give us all things?

Romans 8:32

Tell the righteous it will be well with them, for they will enjoy the fruit of their deeds.

Isaiah 3:10

Surely goodness and love will follow me all the days of my life, and I will dwell in the house of the LORD forever.

Psalms 23:6

Salvation

In reply Jesus declared, "I tell you the truth, unless a man is born again, he cannot see the kingdom of God."

"How can a man be born when he is old?" Nicodemus asked. "Surely he cannot enter a second time into his mother's womb to be born!"

Jesus answered, "I tell you the truth, unless a man is born of water and the Spirit, he cannot enter the kingdom of God. Flesh gives birth to flesh, but the Spirit gives birth to spirit. You should not be surprised at my saying, 'You must be born again.' "

John 3:3-7

Therefore, if anyone is in Christ, he is a new creation; the old has gone, the new has come!

2 Corinthians 5:17

God made him who had no sin to be sin for us, so that in him we might become the righteousness of God.

2 Corinthians 5:21

As for you, you were dead in your transgressions and sins.

Ephesians 2:1

This is good, and pleases God our Savior, who wants all men to be saved and to come to a knowledge of the truth.

1 Timothy 2:3, 4

My dear children, I write this to you so that you will not sin, But if anybody does sin, we have one who speaks to the Father in our defense — Jesus Christ, the Righteous One. He is the atoning sacrifice for our sins, and not only for ours but also for the sins of the whole world.

1 John 2:1, 2

When you were dead in your sins and in the uncircumcision of your sinful nature, God made you alive with Christ. He forgave us all our sins. . . .

Colossians 2:13

This is a trustworthy saying that deserves full acceptance (and for this we labor and strive), that we have put our hope in the living God, who is the Savior of all men, and especially of those who believe.

1 Timothy 4:9, 10

But the gift is not like the trespass. For if the many died by the trespass of the one man, how much more did God's grace and the gift that came by the grace of the one man, Jesus Christ, overflow to the many!

Romans 5:15

But when the kindness and love of God our Savior appeared, he saved us, not because of righteous things we had done, but because of his mercy. He saved us through the washing of rebirth and renewal by the Holy Spirit, whom he poured out on us generously through Jesus Christ our Savior.

Titus 3:4-6

Seeking God

... The LORD is with you when you are with him. If you seek him, he will be found by you, but if you forsake him, he will forsake you.

2 Chronicles 15:2

Sow for yourselves righteousness, reap the fruit of unfailing love, and break up your unplowed ground; for it is time to seek the LORD, until he comes and showers righteousness on you.

Hosea 10:12

And without faith it is impossible to please God, because anyone who comes to him must believe that he exists and that he rewards those who earnestly seek him.

Hebrews 11:6

God did this so that men would seek him and perhaps reach out for him and find him, though he is not far from each one of us.

Acts 17:27

The LORD is good to those whose hope is in him, to the one who seeks him.

Lamentations 3:25

This is what the LORD says to the house of Israel: "Seek me and live."

Amos 5:4

You will seek me and find me when you seek me with all your heart.

Jeremiah 29:13

But if from there you seek the LORD your God, you will find him if you look for him with all your heart and with all your soul.

Deuteronomy 4:29

. . . "The good hand of our God is on everyone who looks to him, but his great anger is against all who forsake him."

Ezra 8:22

"And you, my son Solomon, acknowledge the God of your father, and serve him with wholehearted devotion and with a willing mind, for the LORD searches every heart and understands every motive behind the thoughts. If you seek him, he will be found by you; but if you forsake him, he will reject you forever."

1 Chronicles 28:9

But if you will look to God and plead with the Almighty, if you are pure and upright, even now he will rouse himself on your behalf and restore you to your rightful place.

Job 8:5, 6

Those who know your name will trust in you, for you, LORD, have never forsaken those who seek you.

Psalms 9:10

Self-Denial

Then Jesus said to his disciples, "If anyone would come after me, he must deny himself and take up his cross and follow me. For whoever wants to save his life will lose it, but whoever loses his life for me will find it. What good will it be for a man if he gains the whole world, yet forfeits his soul? Or what can a man give in exchange for his soul?"

Matthew 16:24-26

Therefore, brothers, we have an obligation — but it is not to the sinful nature, to live according to it. For if you live according to the sinful nature, you will die; but if by the Spirit you put to death the misdeeds of the body, you will live.

Romans 8:12, 13

Those who belong to Christ Jesus have crucified the sinful nature with its passions and desires.

Galatians 5:24

For the grace of God that brings salvation has appeared to all men.

It teaches us to say "No" to ungodliness and worldly passions, and to live self-controlled, upright and godly lives in this present age.

Titus 2:11, 12

"I tell you the truth," Jesus said to them, "no one who has left home or wife or brothers or parents or children for the sake of the kingdom of God will fail to receive many times as much in this age and, in the age to come, eternal life."

Luke 18:29, 30

But I tell you, Do not resist an evil person. If someone strikes you on the right cheek, turn to him the other also. And if someone wants to sue you and take your tunic, let him have your cloak as well. If someone forces you to go one mile, go with him two miles.

Matthew 5:39-41

Self-Righteousness

"But you have said in my hearing — I heard the very words — 'I am pure and without sin; I am clean and free from guilt.' "

Job 33:8, 9

"Do you think this is just? You say, 'I will be cleared by God.' "

Job 35:2

Woe to those who are wise in their own eyes and clever in their own sight.

Isaiah 5:21

Indeed, God does not listen to their empty plea; the Almighty pays no attention to it.

Job 35:13

Do you see a man wise in his own eyes? There is more hope for a fool than for him.

Proverbs 26:12

If anyone thinks he is something when he is nothing, he deserves himself.

Galatians 6:3

But, "Let him who boasts boast in the LORD."
For it is not the one who commends himself who is approved, but the one whom the LORD commends.

2 Corinthians 10:17, 18

Jesus said, "If you were blind, you would not be guilty of sin; but now that you claim you can see, your guilt remains."

John 9:41

All of us have become like one who is unclean, and all our righteous acts are like filthy rags; we all shrivel up like a leaf, and like the wind our sins sweep us away.

Isaiah 64:6

A greedy man stirs up dissension, but he who trusts in the LORD will prosper.

He who trusts in himself is a fool, but he who walks in wisdom is kept safe.

Proverbs 28:25, 26

He said to them, "You are the ones who justify yourselves in the eyes of men, but God knows your hearts. What is highly valued among men is detestable in God's sight."

Luke 16:15

Let another praise you, and not your own mouth; someone else, and not your own lips.

Proverbs 27:2

Sexual Sins

. . . The body is not meant for sexual immorality, but for the LORD, and the LORD for the body.

1 Corinthians 6:13

Flee from sexual immortality. All other sins a man commits are outside his body, but he who sins sexually sins against his own body.

Do you not know that your body is a temple of the Holy Spirit, who is in you, whom you have received from God? You are not your own; you were bought at a price. Therefore honor God with your body.

1 Corinthians 6:18-20

Now for the matters you wrote about: It is good for a man not to marry.

1 Corinthians 7:1

Now to the unmarried and the widows I say: It is good for them to stay unmarried, as I am. But if they cannot control themselves, they should marry, for it is better to marry than to burn with passion.

1 Corinthians 7:8, 9

But the man who has settled the matter in his own mind, who is under no compulsion but has control over his own will, and who has made up his mind not to marry the virgin — this man also does the right thing.

1 Corinthians 7:37

No temptation has seized you except what is common to man. And God is faithful; he will not let you be tempted beyond what you can bear. But when you are tempted, he will also provide a way out so that you can stand up under it.

1 Corinthians 10:13

These are those who did not defile themselves with women, for they kept themselves pure. They follow the Lamb wherever he goes. They were purchased from among men and offered as firstfruits to God and the Lamb.

Revelation 14:4

It is God's will that you should be holy: that you should avoid sexual immorality.

1 Thessalonians 4:3

Marriage should be honored by all, and the marriage bed kept pure, for God will judge the adulterer and all the sexually immoral.

Hebrews 13:4

Do you not know that your bodies are members of Christ himself? Shall I then take the members of Christ and unite them with a prostitute? Never!

1 Corinthians 6:15

A wife of noble character who can find? She is worth far more than rubies.

Proverbs 31:10

Because he himself suffered when he was tempted, he is able to help those who are being tempted.

Hebrews 2:18

If this is so, then the Lord knows how to rescue godly men from trials and to hold the unrighteous for the day of judgment, while continuing their punishment.

2 Peter 2:9

Blessed is the man who perseveres under trial, because when he has stood the test, he will receive the crown of life that God has promised to those who love him.

James 1:12

For we do not have a high priest who is unable to sympathize with our weaknesses, but we have one who has been tempted in every way, just as we are — yet was without sin. Let us then approach the throne of grace with confidence, so that we may receive mercy and find grace to help us in our time of need.

Hebrews 4:15, 16

Shame

As the Scripture says, "Everyone who trusts in him will never be put to shame."

Romans 10:11

Then I will not be put to shame when I consider all your commands.

Psalms 119:6

And hope does not disappoint us, because God has poured out his love into our hearts by the Holy Spirit, whom he has given us.

Romans 5:5

That is why I am suffering as I am. Yet I am not ashamed, because I know whom I have believed, and am convinced that he is able to guard what I have entrusted to him for that day.

2 Timothy 1:12

As it is written: "See, I lay in Zion a stone that causes men to stumble and a rock that makes them fall, and the one who trusts in him will never be put to shame."

Romans 9:33

Do your best to present yourself to God as one approved, a workman who does not need to be ashamed and who correctly handles the word of truth.

2 Timothy 2:15

However, if you suffer as a Christian, do not be ashamed, but praise God that you bear that name.

1 Peter 4:16

May my heart be blameless toward your decrees,
that I may not be put to shame.

Psalms 119:80

Sickness

Is any one of you sick? He should call the elders of the church to pray over him and anoint him with oil in the name of the Lord. And the prayer offered in faith will make the sick person well; the Lord will raise him up. If he has sinned, he will be forgiven. Therefore confess your sins to each other and pray for each other so that you may be healed. The prayer of a righteous man is powerful and effective.

James 5:14-16

When he had gone indoors, the blind men came to him, and he asked them, "Do you believe that I am able to do this?"

"Yes, LORD," they replied.

Then he touched their eyes and said, "According to your faith will it be done to you"; and their sight was restored. Jesus warned them sternly, "See that no one knows about this."

Matthew 9:28-30

Heal me, O LORD, and I will be healed; save me and I will be saved, for you are the one I praise.

Jeremiah 17:14

"But so that you may know that the Son of Man has authority on earth to forgive sins. . . ." Then he said to the paralytic, "Get up, take your mat and go home." And the man got up and went home.

Matthew 9:6, 7

Jesus went throughout Galilee, teaching in their synagogues, preaching the good news of the kingdom, and healing every disease and sickness among the people. News about him spread all over Syria, and people brought to him all who were ill with various diseases, those suffering severe pain, the demon-possessed, the epileptics and the paralytics, and he healed them.

Matthew 4:23, 24

"But I will restore you to health and heal your wounds," declares the LORD.

Jeremiah 30:17

Worship the LORD your God, and his blessing will be on your food and water. I will take away sickness from among you.

Exodus 23:25

He himself bore our sins in his body on the tree, so that we might die to sins and live for righteousness; by his wounds you have been healed.

1 Peter 2:24

But he was pierced for our transgressions, he was crushed for our iniquities; the punishment that brought us peace was upon him, and by his wounds we are healed.

Isaiah 53:5

Sin, Freedom From

I will sprinkle clean water on you, and you will be clean; I will cleanse you from all your impurities and from all your idols. I will give you a new heart and put a new spirit in you; I will remove from you your heart of stone and give you a heart of flesh.

Ezekiel 36:25, 26

All the prophets testify about him that everyone who believes in him receives forgiveness of sins through his name.

Acts 10:43

For we know that our old self was crucified with him so that the body of sin might be rendered powerless, that we should no longer be slaves to sin — because anyone who has died has been freed from sin.

Romans 6:6, 7

Therefore, if anyone is in Christ, he is a new creation; the old has gone, the new has come!

2 Corinthians 5:17

What shall we say, then? Shall we go on sinning so that grace may increase? By no means! We died to sin; how can we live in it any longer?

Romans 6:1, 2

In the same way, count yourselves dead to sin but alive to God in Christ Jesus.

Romans 6:11

For sin shall not be your master, because you are not under law, but under grace.

Romans 6:14

Sin, Redemption From

"She will give birth to a son, and you are to give him the name Jesus, because he will save his people from their sins."

Matthew 1:21

"Therefore, my brothers, I want you to know that through Jesus the forgiveness of sins is proclaimed to you."

Acts 13:38

But you know that he appeared so that he might take away our sins. And in him is no sin.

1 John 3:5

. . . But if anyone does sin, we have one who speaks to the Father in our defense — Jesus Christ, the Righteous One. He is the atoning sacrifice for our sins, and not only for ours but also for the sins of the whole world.

1 John 2:1, 2

He himself bore our sins in his body on the tree, so that we might die to sins and live for righteousness; by his wounds you have been healed.

1 Peter 2:24

Here is a trustworthy saying that deserves full acceptance: Christ Jesus came into the world to save sinners — of whom I am the worst.

1 Timothy 1:15

But he was pierced for our transgressions, he was crushed for our iniquities; the punishment that brought us peace was upon him, and by his wounds we are healed.

We all, like sheep, have gone astray, each of us has turned to his own way; and the LORD has laid on him the iniquity of us all.

Isaiah 53:5, 6

The next day John saw Jesus coming toward him and said, "Look, the Lamb of God, who takes away the sin of the world!"

John 1:29

In him we have redemption through his blood, the forgiveness of sins, in accordance with the riches of God's grace.

Ephesians 1:7

Who gave himself for our sins to rescue us from the present evil age, according to the will of our God and Father.

Galatians 1:4

So Christ was sacrificed once to take away the sins of many people; and he will appear a second time, not to bear sin, but to bring salvation to those who are waiting for him.

Hebrews 9:28

Because by one sacrifice he has made perfect forever those who are being made holy.

Hebrews 10:14

Slander and Reproach

"Blessed are you when people insult you, persecute you and falsely say all kinds of evil against you because of me. Rejoice and be glad, because great is your reward in heaven, for in the same way they persecuted the prophets who were before you."

Matthew 5:11, 12

If you are insulted because of the name of Christ, you are blessed, for the Spirit of glory and of God rests on you.

1 Peter 4:14

He sends from heaven and saves me, rebuking those who hotly pursue me;   ***Selah***
God sends his love and his faithfulness.

Psalms 57:3

"Hear me, you who know what is right, you people who have my law in your hearts: Do not fear the reproach of men or be terrified by their insults."

Isaiah 51:7

In the shelter of your presence you hide them from the intrigues of men; in your dwelling you keep them safe from accusing tongues.

Psalms 31:20

You will be protected from the lash of the tongue, and need not fear when destruction comes.

Job 5:21

He will make your righteousness shine like the dawn, the justice of your cause like the noonday sun.

Psalms 37:6

Success

The house of the righteous contains great treasure, but the income of the wicked brings them trouble.

Proverbs 15:6

Humility and the fear of the Lord bring wealth and honor and life.

Proverbs 22:4

Then the Lord your God will make you most prosperous in all the work of your hands and in the fruit of your womb, the young of your livestock and the crops of your land. The Lord will again delight in you and make you prosperous, just as he delighted in your fathers.

Deuteronomy 30:9

He will also send you rain for the seed you sow in the ground, and the food that comes from the land will be rich and plentiful. In that day your cattle will graze in broad meadows.

Isaiah 30:23

That everyone may eat and drink, and find satisfaction in all his toil — this is the gift of God.

Ecclesiastes 3:13

The Lord will open the heavens, the storehouse of his bounty, to send rain on your land in season and to bless all the work of your hands. You will lend to many nations but will borrow from none.

The LORD will make you the head, not the tail. If you pay attention to the commands of the LORD your God that I give you this day and carefully follow them, you will always be at the top, never at the bottom.

Deuteronomy 28:11-13

Moreover, when God gives any man wealth and possessions, and enables him to enjoy them, to accept his lot and be happy in his work — this is a gift of God.

Ecclesiastes 5:19

What you decide on will be done, and light will shine on your ways.

Job 22:28

With me are riches and honor, enduring wealth and prosperity.

My fruit is better than fine gold; what I yield surpasses choice silver.

Proverbs 8:18, 19

Wealth and riches are in his house, and his righteousness endures forever.

Psalms 112:3

And assign your nuggets to the dust, your gold of Ophir to the rocks in the ravines, then the Almighty will be your gold, the choicest silver for you.

Job 22:24, 25

I will provide grass in the fields for your cattle, and you will eat and be satisfied.

Deuteronomy 11:15

You will eat the fruit of your labor; blessings and prosperity will be yours.

Psalms 128:2

They will build houses and dwell in them; they will plant vineyards and eat their fruit.

No longer will they build houses and others live in them, or plant and others eat. For as the days of a tree, so will be the days of my people; my chosen ones will long enjoy the works of their hands.

They will not toil in vain or bear children doomed to misfortune; for they will be a people blessed by the LORD, they and their descendants with them.

Isaiah 65:21-23

All these blessings will come upon you and accompany you if you obey the LORD your God:

You will be blessed in the city and blessed in the country.

The fruit of your womb will be blessed, and the crops of your land and the young of your livestock — the calves of your herds and the lambs of your flocks.

Your basket and your kneading trough will be blessed.

You will be blessed when you come in and blessed when you go out.

Deuteronomy 28:2-6

Trust

God is our refuge and strength, an ever present help in trouble. Therefore we will not fear, though the earth give way and the mountains fall into the heart of the sea.

Psalms 46:1, 2

For the Lord God is a sun and shield; the Lord bestows favor and honor; no good thing does he withhold from those whose walk is blameless.

O Lord Almighty, blessed is the man who trusts in you.

Psalms 84:11, 12

Trust in the Lord and do good; dwell in the land and enjoy safe pasture.

Delight yourself in the Lord and he will give you the desires of your heart.

Commit your way to the Lord; trust in him and he will do this.

Psalms 37:3-5

Trust in the Lord with all your heart and lean not on your own understanding; in all your ways acknowledge him, and he will make your paths straight.

Proverbs 3:5, 6

"Do not be afraid, little flock, for your Father has been pleased to give you the kingdom."

Luke 12:32

So do not worry, saying, "What shall we eat?" or "What shall we drink?" or "What shall we wear?" For the pagans run after all these things, and your heavenly Father knows that you need them.

Matthew 6:31, 32

Cast all your anxiety on him because he cares for you.

1 Peter 5:7

Blessed is the man who makes the LORD his trust. . . .

Psalms 40:4

Those who trust in the LORD are like Mount Zion, which cannot be shaken but endures forever.

Psalms 125:1

Wisdom

If any of you lacks wisdom, he should ask God, who gives generously to all without finding fault, and it will be given to him.

James 1:5

. . . He will teach us his ways, so that we may walk in his paths. . . .

Isaiah 2:3

I will instruct you and teach you in the way you should go; I will counsel you and watch over you.

Psalms 32:8

To the man who pleases him, God gives wisdom, knowledge and happiness. . . .

Ecclesiastes 2:26

I will praise the LORD, who counsels me; even at night my heart instructs me.

Psalms 16:7

Then you will understand the fear of the LORD and find the knowledge of God.
For the LORD gives wisdom, and from his mouth come knowledge and understanding.
He holds victory in store for the upright, he is a shield to those whose walk is blameless.

Proverbs 2:5-7

Surely you desire truth in the inner parts; you teach me wisdom in the inmost place.

Psalms 51:6

We know also that the Son of God has come and has given us understanding, so that we may know him who is true. And we are in him who is true — even in his Son Jesus Christ. He is the true God and eternal life.

1 John 5:20

For God, who said, "Let light shine out of darkness," made his light shine in our hearts to give us the light of the knowledge of the glory of God in the face of Christ.

2 Corinthians 4:6

Evil men do not understand justice, but those who seek the LORD understand it fully.

Proverbs 28:5

Word of God

I am not ashamed of the gospel, because it is the power of God for the salvation of everyone who believes. . . .

Romans 1:16

Blessed is the one who reads the words of this prophecy, and blessed are those who hear it and take to heart what is written in it, because the time is near.

Revelation 1:3

And we have the word of the prophets made more certain, and you will do well to pay attention to it, as to a light shining in a dark place, until the day dawns and the morning star rises in your hearts.

2 Peter 1:19

The word of God is living and active. Sharper than any double-edged sword, it penetrates even to dividing soul and spirit, joints and marrow; it judges the thoughts and attitudes of the heart.

Hebrews 4:12

The entrance of your words gives light; it gives understanding to the simple.

Psalms 119:130

For these commands are a lamp, this teaching is a light, and the corrections of discipline are the way to life.

Proverbs 6:23

Your word is a lamp to my feet and a light for my path.

Psalms 119:105

You diligently study the Scriptures because you think that by them you possess eternal life. These are the Scriptures that testify about me.

John 5:39

. . . the holy Scriptures, which are able to make you wise for salvation through faith in Christ Jesus. All Scripture is God-breathed and is useful for teaching, rebuking, correcting and training and righteousness.

2 Timothy 3:15, 16

Consequently, faith comes from hearing the message, and the message is heard through the word of Christ.

Romans 10:17

Like newborn babies, crave pure spiritual milk, so that by it you will grow up in your salvation.

1 Peter 2:2

Fix these words of mine in your hearts and minds; tie them as symbols on your hands and bind them on your foreheads.

Deuteronomy 11:18

Do not let this Book of the Law depart from your mouth; meditate on it day and night, so that you may be careful to do everything written in it. Then you will be prosperous and successful.

Joshua 1:8

Therefore, get rid of all moral filth and the evil that is so prevalent and humbly accept the word planted in you, which can save you.

Do not merely listen to the word, and so deceive yourselves. Do what it says. Anyone who listens to the word but does not do what it says is like a man who looks at his face in a mirror and, after looking at himself, goes away and immediately forgets what he looks like. But the man who looks intently into the perfect law that gives freedom, and continues to do this, not forgetting what he has heard, but doing it — he will be blessed in what he does.

James 1:21-25

For you have been born again, not of perishable seed, but of imperishable, through the living and enduring word of God.

1 Peter 1:23

"Now I commit you to God and to the word of his grace, which can build you up and give you an inheritance among all those who are sanctified."

Acts 20:32

NOTES

NOTES

NOTES

NOTES